Secretarial Practice Made Simple

Revised Edition

Betty Hutchinson and Carol Milano

Edited and prepared for publication by The Stonesong Press, Inc.

A MADE SIMPLE BOOK

DOUBLEDAY

NEW YORK   LONDON   TORONTO   SYDNEY   AUCKLAND

Edited and prepared for publication by The Stonesong Press
Managing Editor: Sheree Bykofsky
Design: Blackbirch Graphics, Inc.
Editorial Consultant: Magdalin Leonardo

A MADE SIMPLE BOOK

Published by Doubleday, a division of
Bantam Doubleday Dell Publishing Group, Inc.
666 Fifth Avenue, New York, New York 10103

MADE SIMPLE and DOUBLEDAY are trademarks of Doubleday,
a division of Bantam Doubleday Dell Publishing
Group, Inc.

Library of Congress Cataloging-in-Publication Data
Hutchinson, Betty.
   Secretarial practice made simple/by Betty Hutchinson and
Carol Milano—Rev. ed.
   A MADE SIMPLE BOOK
   ISBN 0-385-41428-5
   1. Office practice. I. Milano, Carol. II. Title.
HF5547.5.H88 1990
651.3'741—dc20

—   90-3143
CIP

CONTENTS

INTRODUCTION *11*

PART ONE: THE RIGHT BEGINNING
Chapter 1: **First Days**
        Your Job Description *17*
        A Word of Caution *18*
        Learn the Company *18*
        Policies and Procedures *19*
        Learn Your Boss's Job *20*
        Loyalty, Gossip, and Dress *21*

PART TWO: WITH THE OUTSIDE WORLD
Chapter 2: **Telephone**
        Telephone Manner *26*
        Answering the Telephone *27*
        Telephone Messages *27*

If Your Boss Is Away   *28*

Interrupting Your Boss for a Call   *28*

Making Outgoing Calls   *29*

The Telephone Power Game   *29*

"Is He In?"   *30*

"I'll Transfer You"   *30*

Get the Number Right   *30*

Ending a Call   *30*

"Hello"   *31*

"I'll Put You on Hold"   *31*

Managing Voice Mail   *31*

Complex Phone Systems   *31*

Chapter 3:   **Reception**

Kinds of Visits   *33*

Confirm the Appointment   *36*

Who Makes the Appointment   *36*

Keeping the Master Appointment Calendar   *36*

Company Visitors   *37*

A Tactful Guardian of the Door   *37*

A Note About Out-of-Town Visitors   *38*

Chapter 4:   **Correspondence**

Incoming Correspondence   *39*

A Correspondence List   *41*

Marking the Letter   *41*

Matters You Can Handle   *42*

Outgoing Correspondence   *42*

Salutation   *45*

Body of the Letter   *46*

Conclusion   *46*

Complimentary Closing   *46*

Dictator/Secretary   *47*

Copies and Enclosures   *47*

Handwritten Correspondence   *50*

Presentation for Signature   *50*

Accuracy   *51*

Chapter 5: **The Facsimile (Fax) Machine**
Fax Etiquette   *53*
Keeping Logs of Documents   *54*
Learning Your Own Firm's Procedures   *54*
How the Fax Machine Works   *54*
Monitoring Fax Paper Supply   *54*
Keeping Machine On or Off   *55*
Junk Fax   *55*

Chapter 6: **Reservations**
Travel   *56*
Reconfirmation   *58*
VIP Airline Clubs   *58*
Frequent-Flyer Programs   *59*
Meals   *59*
Rental Cars   *59*
Hotels   *60*
Restaurants   *60*
A Small Business Lunch   *62*
Entertainment   *62*

Chapter 7: **Express Services**
Messenger   *64*
Couriers   *65*
Express Mail   *65*
United Parcel Service   *65*
Overnight Air-Express Service   *66*
International   *67*
Airlines   *67*
Telegrams and Electronic Mail   *68*

Chapter 8: **International Correspondence**
Characteristics of Language Use   *70*
Users of English as a Second Language   *71*
British English   *73*
A Sample Letter   *74*

PART THREE: INSIDE THE COMPANY

Chapter 9:   **Dictation**
              Pool Dictation   *78*
              Beginning Worries   *78*
              First Copy as Final Copy   *79*
              First Copy as Draft Copy   *79*
              Dictating Reference Needs   *79*
              Final Form   *80*
              Retention of Original   *80*
              Punctuation   *80*
              Enclosures   *80*
              Distribution of Copies   *81*
              Spare Batteries   *81*
              Soundalike Words   *81*
              Correction Marks   *82*

Chapter 10:   **Your Boss's Calendar**
              The Importance of Time   *83*
              Who Keeps the Master Calendar   *83*
              The Day in Fifteen-Minute Segments   *84*
              In-Company Visitors   *84*
              Outside Visitors   *84*
              Tentative Appointments   *85*
              When Your Boss Is Running Late   *85*
              Who Should Know About Your Boss's Schedule   *86*
              Appointment Courtesies   *86*
              Appointments with Juniors   *86*
              Appointments with Peers and Seniors   *87*

Chapter 11:   **Office Appearance**   *88*

Chapter 12:   **Dress for Success**   *91*

Chapter 13:   **Guarding the Door**   *94*

Chapter 14: **Routines and Reminder Systems**
Routines   *96*
Reminder Suggestions   *97*
Daily Reminder Notes   *98*

Chapter 15: **Memos**
Direct Style for Memo Writing   *100*
Types of Memos   *100*
Forms for Writing Memos   *101*
File Copies   *101*
Elements in a Memo   *102*
Your Memos   *102*
Sample Memos   *103*

Chapter 16: **Reports**   *106*

Chapter 17: **Financial Statements**   *113*

Chapter 18: **Meetings**
Agenda   *117*
Reports and Financial Statements   *118*
Physical Arrangements   *118*
If You Attend the Meeting   *119*
Minutes of the Meeting   *119*
Follow-Up After the Meeting   *120*
The Next Meeting   *120*

Chapter 19: **Filing**
The Keeper of the File   *121*
The File as an Ongoing Record   *121*
Learn the Files   *122*
Respect the Files   *122*
Introduce Any Changes to the Files Slowly and Cautiously   *122*
Housekeeping   *123*
Originals of Contracts and Agreements   *123*

Confidential Information   *123*
Space for Files   *124*
Microfilming Files   *124*
Files and the File Clerk   *124*
Cross-Referencing Files   *125*
Filing Suggestions   *125*

Chapter 20:   **The Automated Office**
Records Management   *126*
Editing   *127*
Computer Back-Up Procedures   *128*
The Myth of the "Paperless Office"   *128*
Monitoring Information on Disks   *128*
Working with LANs   *128*
Workstations with Shared Equipment   *128*
The Versatile Modem   *129*
Coping with Today's Faster Pace   *130*
Lighting and Office Furniture   *130*
Automated Postage Meters   *131*
About Meters and Scales   *131*
Using Postage Charts   *131*
Keeping Copier Logs   *131*
Training Courses   *132*
Working with a Computer Consultant   *132*
Getting Service for Software, Hardware, Phone, or Fax   *132*
Creating Envelopes on Your PC   *133*
What Else Can Your Computer Do?   *133*
Keeping Up with New Developments   *133*

PART FOUR: LETTER AND MEMO SKILLS
Chapter 21:   **Grammar and Sentence Structure**   *136*

Chapter 22:   **Spelling**   *140*

Chapter 23:   **Word Division**   *145*

Chapter 24: **Compound Words**
Compound Words   *148*
Words with Prefixes   *153*

Chapter 25: **Abbreviations**
Latin Abbreviations   *155*
Company Names and Organizations   *156*
Titles and Forms of Address   *157*
Metric Abbreviations   *158*
English Abbreviations   *158*
Geography and Locations   *158*
Time   *158*

Chapter 26: **Postal Service Forms**
Express Mail   *161*
Return Receipt   *162*
Registered Mail   *162*
Certified Mail   *162*
Insured Mail   *163*
Collect-on-Delivery (COD) Mail   *163*
Special Delivery   *164*
Special Handling   *164*
Customs Declarations   *164*
Zip-Code Directory   *165*

Chapter 27: **Secretarial Organizations and Associations**   *166*

INDEX   *169*

After an extensive study of America's labor force, the U.S. Government projects in its *Occupational Outlook Handbook* (1989) that "well-qualified secretaries will be in great demand in the 1990s and beyond, and should find many job opportunities." In 1986, secretaries held over 3,234,000 positions in the United States. The field remains one of America's largest occupational groups.

"Many employers complain of a shortage of first-rate secretaries," notes the *Occupational Outlook Handbook*. "A large number of job openings will arise through the year 2000 due to replacement needs." Every year, several hundred thousand secretaries leave the work force, because of retirement, maternity, promotion, illness, or other reasons. This means a vast number of people will find employment as secretaries throughout the 1990s and into the next century.

This book was written using the following points to guide what was covered and how it was expressed.

1. A secretary is a professional. As a professional, you may want to perform the many and varied responsibilities of secretarial work with competence, confidence, and style.

2. Some secretaries will move to different responsibilities in a company—often becoming executives themselves; others will look on their secretarial job as "something to do" while waiting for something else to come up. The great majority of secretaries

know the worth of what they do and want to increase their level of professionalism. Whichever kind of secretary you are—one with hopes of something greater that might come from your job, one passing through, or one for whom it is a chosen career—*Secretarial Practice Made Simple* will help you raise the level of work you do as a secretary. This will benefit your company and your boss, while making your life at the office easier, more satisfying, and rewarding.

3. Both females and males are splendid secretaries. Since you may be either a man or a woman, the discussion of services you can perform to smooth the work and life of your boss is not related to sexist roles or stereotypes.

4. Skilled executives can be either female or male. We do not assume your boss is a man. In one chapter we refer to the boss as "her," in the next as "him." We find that smoother than the "him or her" or "she/he" styles some writers use. We wish the English language offered a word with fewer emotional overtones than "boss," but all the known alternatives seem even less satisfactory or too restricted.

5. The office environment has changed rapidly, with the introduction of higher-tech communications devices, ranging from electronic typewriters and word processors to personal computers and fax machines. Not all offices, nor all executives, have embraced this technology, and no level of application is standard. But the technology steadily—and increasingly—affects a secretary's work. We discuss new environments and equipment where appropriate. If you work in an up-to-date office, these comments will make sense to you; if your office does not yet use newer means of communication, they will alert you to what is prob-

ably soon coming your way. The silicon chip is changing the office scene every bit as much as the Remington typewriter did a century ago.

6. Many secretarial handbooks contain extensive lists of words, grammatical rules, proper forms of address, and the like, with a selected list of reference books included. In this book, however, we concentrate on how to perform the many services in a secretarial job description, rather than focus on language usage.

7. The list of tasks a secretary must perform is extensive. *Secretarial Practice Made Simple* covers the primary tasks you undertake each day. One mark of a skilled professional secretary is the ability to move from one task to another instantly and easily. You may wish to have every minute of your day preplanned and fully under your control. But it just doesn't work that way. As you are well into a pressing task, you may be interrupted by the telephone, visitors, unexpected job assignments from your boss—sometimes of an urgent nature because things come up that no one expected when the day began. You must handle these secretarial roles with flexibility and grace, while continuing to carry through on your known priorities and routines.

8. To grow in professional competence, you will need to develop some skills you may not now have or may have only in part. Critical skills and knowledge to acquire or strengthen include typing, word processing, possibly shorthand or speed writing, language usage, and general office procedures. I suggest ways for you to gain additional training (with a word of caution about the value of such training compared with on-the-job development and guided professional reading). The exact areas you need to

develop depend entirely on you and your background, the nature of the work you do, and your ambitions. This book gives an overall introduction to career enrichment, but you need to tailor-make it for yourself.

The secretary I had in mind as I wrote this book was a composite of several people I have worked with, hired and trained, or sought from other departments to work with me. Some of these people are college graduates; some entered the work force right out of high school. Some of them had always wanted to be excellent secretaries; that role in the company was the career goal they had set for themselves. Others wanted quite a different ultimate career, but worked as secretaries to support themselves and to gain experience in an office environment or in a particular company or industry. Many of these people moved in the career direction of their choice because they were spotted by someone in the company who recognized they were responsible workers. Others were transferred to the areas they wanted to be in because I valued them and the excellent work they had done for me and recommended their promotion. Whichever you are—one who wants a secretarial career or one who wants to be a good secretary as part of preparing for the next step—you will be able to serve your career, your boss, and the company better by putting into practice the suggestions you find in this book.

Most importantly, you spend about one third of each twenty-four-hour working day in your office. That's too much of your time and energy to take casually. You should be basically happy with what you do and the people with whom you work. *Secretarial Practice Made Simple* is intended to enable you to feel good about the work you do—to help you do it well and with personal satisfaction. You will contribute to a good working relationship with your boss and your colleagues when you do your work professionally and enjoy that sense of accomplishment. That good working relationship, in turn, will make it easier to do your job skillfully.

In the course of my own working life, I have been an office worker, a secretary, an executive secretary, an assistant to a chief executive officer of a large international firm, a supervisor of secretarial services in a large corporation, an executive with my own secretary, and have founded my own company and serve as its president. It is my strong conviction that business and industry cannot exist without secretarial expertise performed with sensitivity and good judgment. *Secretarial Practice Made Simple* contains what I tried to be, what I trained many to become, and what I want to have in colleagues who work with me. The specific advice is simple. It is the work of a lifetime to keep growing and meeting the challenges of new opportunities.

Betty Hutchinson, 1985
revised by Carol Milano, 1990

PART ONE

THE RIGHT BEGINNING

Whether you are an experienced secretary facing a new company or a new boss, or a beginner starting your first assignment, several essential principles should be foremost in your mind during the first few weeks. These are basic guidelines about what you do, how you do it, and how you relate to other people in the company.

First Days

Let's first consider, "What is a secretary?" The dictionary gives some leads, but touches only the main points. It refers to someone who handles correspondence, maintains records and files, and ensures that numerous details are taken care of in the efficient running of an office. In some instances, the secretary—often called a "general secretary"—is the officer who administers an organization, such as the United Nations, or a governmental department, such as the Secretary of State. In many countries, the senior civil service officers are called "Permanent Secretaries," as contrasted with "Ministers," who change with the varying political winds.

This more administrative note in the secretarial role suggests strongly that your job can be a blend of caring for the paperwork flow of your boss and, at the same time, doing whatever is helpful in enabling him to better administer his work. The more you develop these administrative skills, the more he will probably delegate routine administrative tasks to you. Unlike an assistant executive, you do not have your own line of command in an organizational chart; rather, you serve as an extension of your boss, allowing him to concentrate on major matters while you handle routines and details for him.

Your Job Description

The most important aspect of your job description is to make sure that you and your boss have the same concept of what your job is. If he thinks of you as a monitor of the paper chase, he will resist and probably resent your efforts to help relieve him of administrative routines. On the other hand, if he wants you to be responsible for administrative routines, while you consider yourself the caretaker of all correspondence and files, he will feel you are falling down on the job and failing to meet his expectations. Before long he will start looking for someone who can "really help" him, leaving you to wonder what went wrong because you thought you were doing the job well.

In your initial interview or during your first day on the job, ask to talk with your boss about what you both want the job to be. He may never have had a secretary before, or may never have employed one for more than restricted, paper-centered tasks. The idea that you can relieve him of many time-consuming routine tasks may be a new one.

Your boss may be eager for help, but prefer to transfer matters to you slowly, to see how easily you can assume them before assigning you more. By talking about your respective expectations, and about time periods during which you learn certain parts of the job before being given more, you will find yourselves working together in defining your job. This is much better than your both having to guess at what you each expect of the other—and never really guessing entirely right.

This kind of discussion early in your relationship will help establish a freedom in being able to talk openly and frankly about work matters. In many ways, you will be his eyes and ears in the company, just because you will see and hear things at a level he does not. When you sense something he should be aware of that can affect his performance, it helps if you have already established the ability to talk about business matters in a direct manner.

Sometimes your boss may tell you about some project he is working on that others in the company do not as yet know about; he wants your help in performing the task, and needs to know that you will keep it confidential. Here again, a direct relationship of openness about the nature of your work—established right at the beginning—makes it much easier later on to trust each other with important business matters.

Tip

Ask for a job description. Then make sure that both you and your boss share the same concept of what your job should be.

A Word of Caution

It's important that you like and respect your boss. This does not mean you have to like everything about him or raise the level of respect to adoration. But unless you basically like and respect the person you work for, trouble is ahead for both of you. The primary function of your job is to help your boss do his job better. He, in turn, must develop confidence in you and your abilities so that he trusts you with his work (which is also his career). Without mutual respect and confidence, things cannot work out well for either of you. If you have given the job a reasonable try, but the feeling of comfortable interdependence is not there, we suggest you seek a change to another boss or another company.

Learn the Company

Next to establishing mutual expectations and a relationship of openness with your boss, the most important first task is to learn the primary business of the company and how the firm carries out that business. Professional management analysts call the main business of a company its "mission." This mission may be expressed in a single sentence, or it may take several paragraphs. Your boss has a specific job in the company to enable it to achieve its mission. His work is the company's work; the better he attains part of the company's goals, the more responsibilities he will be given to complete more of the company's mission. His work cannot be separated from the company's goals.

Here are some practical ways for you to learn what the company is about:

1. Ask for literature produced by the company that describes its mission, achievements, and plans for the future. Annual reports provide a clear summary, as do employee brochures and magazine articles about the company. If you have a couple of weeks after being hired but before starting your job, ask your new boss-to-be or the company's personnel director for any literature that can help orient you to the company.

2. Soon after you start working together, ask your boss to tell you what the company is all about—its history, its structure, its mission, its policies, and its future. Not only does he know a great deal about it, but it is essential that you see it through his eyes. As you learn more about the company through working there, you may not always see it as he sees it; but it is still vital that you understand his perspective in order to support him in his work.

3. Talk with others over coffee breaks and at lunch about their understanding of the

---

Tip

Unless you basically like and respect the person you work for, great difficulties are sure to arise.

> **Tip**
>   The mission is what the company does; policies and procedures are how the company goes about doing it.

mission and purpose of the company. The lower in the company's organization, the more limited an employee's perspective, so sift out what is important. From fellow employees, you will learn things about what really guides the company that are not written down in the more formal mission and policy statements.

4. From time to time, ask someone outside the company—often someone who does business with the company—what he thinks the purpose and nature of the company are. This person will undoubtedly not know as much as you do about the company, but sometimes you get so close to it that it helps to hear someone comment who is not as personally involved.

5. As you do your own work for your boss, ask yourself once a month how this particular task relates to the company's overall mission. When you do this, you may understand more than you did before about what the company is trying to do. Certainly you will better understand how your boss's work contributes to the company's goals.

Policies and Procedures

As you develop a comprehensive understanding of the mission of the company, you will also gain a grasp of the company's policies and procedures. The mission is what the company does; policies and procedures are how the company goes about doing it. Many companies have written lists of policies and procedures, which may be updated periodically. However, two kinds of policies and procedures not included in any written compilation: those adopted since the last publication, and those that form the all-important "unwritten" policies understood and followed by everyone who has worked within the company for a long time. Being "unwritten" means they cannot be found in any personnel memo or brochure.

Every organization develops its own personality, its own ways of doing things, its own system of unofficial rewards and punishments, its own standards of assessing good and bad performance, its own net-

> **Tip**
>   Your overall loyalty must be to the company; your immediate loyalty must be to your boss.

work of people who really get things done regardless of who the official organization chart shows is responsible for a task. Success in your job calls for you to play an active role in making things happen on behalf of your boss, rather than accepting a passive role in which you are merely told what to do and when. You'll need to learn how to do things in the company way—according to both the formally stated policies and procedures, and the unwritten ones that really govern how things work from day to day.

Unwritten Policies and Procedures

You learn the unwritten policies and procedures by asking your boss how to go about accomplishing a certain task, who to see, and when to see them. You should also ask some of the people who have been around the company for a while and who are on a more or less equal level with you.

Your Workplace Network

In time you will learn who is in your effective working network. It may not turn out to be the same people your boss mentions, since he will tend to think at a higher corporate level than is really appropriate for your own work. You will soon develop a network among the secretaries just as he has built one among the executives. Each network helps accomplish tasks; the choice of the right network depends on the nature of the task to be done.

Learn Your Boss's Job

In order to succeed, learn as much as you can about your boss's job. He is responsible

for certain kinds of work, which may use a technical or professional vocabulary. You need to become familiar with this specialized vocabulary, to have a good idea of the processes or steps implied in these terms, and to understand how their use fits in with your boss's responsibility. Often when he is out of the office or not readily available, someone will call about a letter or memo he wrote, asking for clarification or further elaboration. The more you know about what your boss does, the better you will be able to provide correct and timely information if he cannot do so immediately. When you are not absolutely certain about any information you provide in his absence, make that clear to a visitor or caller, indicate you will refer the matter to your boss for confirmation when he returns, and leave the boss a brief memo about the matter. That way he knows what you've done and can decide whether further steps are needed. A memo insures your boss will not be surprised when a caller later refers to his conversation with you.

Ask the Boss

To learn about your boss's job, ask him when you come across something new you don't understand. Read books and magazine articles he can recommend to you, and seek out information on your own from the company or public library. Do not expect to become an overnight expert, but steadily increase your familiarity with the nature of the job you are helping him to perform.

Ask Other People

You also need to learn about the people with whom your boss deals. Some are in the company; others are outside—vendors,

---

Tip

The best response to gossip is to ignore it. Determine from the first day to gain a reputation as a nongossiper.

---

customers, consultants, professional associates, and colleagues in the same general line of work. He will give you information about who's who. You should quickly learn which callers to put through instantly, and who he can more easily call back. Your caller may also give you a clue to the urgency of the call.

Study the Files

An excellent way of beginning right at the start to learn about the company, your boss's role within it, and who he does a lot of business with both inside and outside the company is to read the files of his correspondence. Start with the most recent and work backward. This is not only an efficient way to gain information, but also shows you how the files are set up and gives you an overall familiarity with the range of business. Right from the beginning your boss will ask you for certain files. A secretary hears, "Bring me the file" more often than any other request. When you pull that file, glance through it so you have some idea about the history of the situation, and a better understanding of what is going on at present and what will be taking place in the days ahead. Make sure everything is in the file that should be there. The file becomes the written record of a series of transactions, developments, problems, achievements, and relationships. You will develop your own ongoing mental file of the situ-

ation, but the physical file is the best available record to refresh your and your boss's memories about the situation. Learn your files from the beginning.

Loyalty, Gossip, and Dress

Three personal matters are sufficiently important to be considered at the very beginning of your work as a secretary: loyalty, gossip, and dress.

Office Politics and Loyalty

Every continuing group of people develops a political character. Your office is no exception. Your boss is a part of the political process in getting things done in the company. He responds in certain ways to his superiors, to those who work under his direct supervision, to those whom he must influence but cannot control, and to those who make up the rest of the executive and staff work force in the company. "Politics" in this sense is not a negative word; it simply describes the fact that people have to learn how best to relate to each other to accomplish a common purpose, while at the same time meeting as best they can their own personal needs for recognition and advancement.

In any political environment, the participants are called on for loyalty to the cause and to the leaders. With other players in the game besides your boss, a company has many centers of loyalty. Although your overall dedication is to the company, your immediate loyalty must be to your boss. Your efforts should be directed to helping him do his work in the best possible manner, alerting him to any problems you sense, and suggesting ways in which you can relieve him of routine chores so he can devote himself more completely to his professional and executive tasks.

Loyalty is a two-way street. As you continue to demonstrate your loyalty to your boss, he will most likely reciprocate in kind. As he moves around or up in the company, you could well move with him, since he appreciates loyal and competent support. Or he can assure that your future in the company is advanced (since he will speak well of you to others, including the personnel officer), even though he may not be able to take you along as his secretary when he goes to his new assignment.

Gossip

Wherever people continue in an ongoing relationship, talk is inevitable. Talk can readily become gossip. In every office are some people who love to gossip. In this sense, "gossip" is defined as idle talk, usually of a personal nature about others, often focused on rumors and speculation, generally of a negative, critical nature rather than positive and supportive. You might be the object of gossip; so, too, might your boss. The best response to gossip is to ignore it. Get busy with something else when you are invited to participate in gossip, say nothing about your boss, and become known as one who is not interested in the gossip mill. Offices all have nongossipers as well as gossipers, who are accepted for what they are. Just determine right from the beginning to gain a reputation as a nongossiper. Your boss will soon learn that you have not joined the gossip clique, and this will reinforce his loyalty to you.

Your Appearance and Dress

Loyalty and handling gossip is a matter of attitude; how you look is a reflection of you as an individual. Few companies these days have what used to be called a "dress code." Even though there may be no rules about what you wear or how much makeup, perfume, or after-shave lotion to apply, let your common sense guide you. Your appearance tells others what you think about yourself. If you dress sloppily, others will readily come to the conclusion that you are a sloppy person in your work and in your confidences. Both you and your boss will be hurt by such a perception. Styles of dress vary from region to region in the country, from

---

Tip

Basic knowledge about your company, your boss's job, the people he regularly deals with, an attitude of loyalty, a determination to be a nongossiper, an appropriate appearance: these are assets of great value. With them, you are well on the way to being a successful secretary.

industry to industry within a region, and from office to office within a company.

What is appropriate dress for a secretary of a new junior executive on the third floor may not be at all appropriate for the president's secretary in the executive suite. Avoid drawing attention to yourself by either overdressing or underdressing to an extreme. Understate your clothes, but with classical choices. Your appearance will then say to your boss, to his bosses, and to your coworkers that you are a professional who is focused on doing the job well. It's advisable to save your "fun" clothes for after-work entertainment. You can certainly dress up to the level of importance appropriate to the responsibility held by your boss.

The great assets are: 1) basic knowledge about your company, your boss's job, the people he regularly deals with; 2) an attitude of loyalty; 3) a determination to be a nongossiper; 4) a pleasing, appropriate appearance. Once you acquire these, you are on the way to being a successful secretary.

PART TWO

WITH THE OUTSIDE WORLD

One whole set of your secretarial relationships is with the world outside the company. In some of these relationships, you are an extension or agent of your boss. In others you are the sole contact a person will have with your company or your boss. In some you handle routine affairs; in others you can make or break your company's future with an outside person or firm. Part II focuses on the range of relationships you have with people outside your company.

CHAPTER TWO

Telephone

The telephone will be your main contact with people beyond your own immediate office—either outside the company or in other departments and sections of the firm. This is true whether the calls are incoming—people seeking you or your boss—or outgoing—placing calls for your boss or making inquiries on her behalf.

Telephone Manner

Your telephone technique and manner give the caller a picture of the kind of person you are, what your boss is like, and the style of office you both run. In fact, for many callers those telephone conversations are the only personal relationship they ever have with you and your boss. Impressions created from the way those calls are handled affect business relationships with your company very directly.

Pleasant and Unhurried Manner

A vital contribution you can make is a pleasant and unhurried manner on the telephone. No matter how rushed and hassled you are when the telephone rings, stop what you are doing, wait one more ring while you take a breath and compose yourself, and then answer the phone in a mood of helpfulness. You don't want to give the caller the impression that this call is an imposition. He should not bear the brunt of any problem you might be experiencing at the mo-

---

Tip

Your telephone technique and manner give the caller a picture of the kind of person you are, the type of individual your boss is, and the style of office you both run. Your most important contribution is a pleasant and unhurried manner on the telephone.

---

ment. Another benefit from pausing a moment is that your voice will automatically lower in tone. If you're tense, your voice is higher and more strident, less pleasant for the caller.

Answering the Telephone

Your boss may want the phone to be answered in a particular way. Ask if that is so. If not, a good way of answering the phone (if your boss's name is Miss Smith) is: "Good morning (afternoon). This is Miss Smith's office. Jane (John) Dow speaking. May I help you?" This answer achieves several things right at the beginning. It creates an initial cordial relationship; "Good morning" is more personal and courteous than a mere "Hello?" The answer also identifies the office immediately to the caller. If the switchboard has plugged in a call for Mr. Jones to your extension by mistake, the caller can correct the matter without taking any more of your (or his) time. You have let the caller know that Jane (John) Dow is ready to assist him, so he can start in at once to explain why he is calling. Try to use the caller's name at least once in the conversation; this confirms that you got it right, and you always flatter someone when you use his name.

Telephone Messages

If the caller asks to talk to Miss Smith, several scenarios are possible. It might be that Miss Smith is out of town and will not return to the office until next Monday. You need not explain to the caller whether Miss Smith is away on business, where she is, or whether she is on vacation. Miss Smith's private and business affairs are not a matter for general conversation over the phone. Ask for the caller's name, telephone number, and reason for wanting to talk with Miss Smith. Indicate that Miss Smith will return the call after she returns. An easy method of getting all the needed information in a convenient form for your boss is to use one of the prepared telephone message pads. One form, manufactured by 3M Company, has a slightly adhesive edge that allows it to stick to even a vertical surface. Other forms have similar spaces for information, but not the adhesive edging. These telephone message pads are readily available in stationery and office-supply stores; your own supply department may buy them in bulk.

Write all the information the form requests: name of the person to whom the message is directed (normally your boss); date and time; name of the person from whom the message comes; caller's company and phone number; whether message came by phone or in person; who is to call whom next; whether the matter is urgent; any short message to be given to your boss; name or initial of person taking the call, so your boss may ask any follow-up question before returning the call.

Your most important contribution is a pleasant and unhurried manner on the telephone.

Having this information about the calls that came in while she was out, and who they were from, gives your boss some choice in setting priorities on returning the calls. She can also ask for files and other information before placing a call, ensuring that she has all the information she needs before she responds. The messages may include calls from her boss, from important customers or clients, from callers who stress urgency and the need to return their calls promptly, or notes about issues you know are critical. If the caller has to be contacted by a certain day or time, be sure to highlight that information for your boss.

If Your Boss Is Away

If your boss is away from the office for several days, the pile of little telephone-message notes might become confusing and create too much clutter. Instead, you can type up a list of calls by day, using columns for the information:

> Calls on February 7, 1999
> From   Phone   Comments

You can place in the "comments" column any particular information about calling back, or messages given to you for your boss. This system organizes all the February 7 calls for her to scan through, allowing her to take whatever action she needs to in light of all the other matters she must attend to after an absence. Prepare similar sheets of paper for her February 8 and February 9 calls.

Interrupting Your Boss for a Call

Some executives prefer you take information on all incoming calls—except those from her boss—and then set aside time to return those calls once or twice a day. These executives have chosen not to have their work interrupted constantly by incoming calls. If she chooses to manage the telephone this way—and we feel it gives her better control over how she utilizes her day—you should tell the caller that Miss Smith is not available at present, but will return the call later that morning (afternoon). If the caller is traveling and will not

---

Tip
Develop a list of regularly called telephone numbers.

have ready access to a telephone, get the best available number for the next day or two. Most calls are not so earthshaking that another day or so is critical. If the caller insists he has to talk with your boss this very day, ask him to wait a minute while you find out whether Miss Smith is now free. Put him on hold, and give your boss the message. If your boss still does not want to talk to the caller just then, tell the caller how very sorry you are that Miss Smith is not available to receive his call at the moment. It is then up to the caller to leave a telephone number or state that he will call again later.

If a Visitor Is in Your Boss's Office

If your boss is seeing a visitor in her office, it is irksome and discourteous for your boss to receive a continual flow of incoming calls while the visitor waits to complete a sentence. Work out with your boss which kinds of calls are urgent enough to interrupt if a visitor is in the office.

Making Outgoing Calls

You will also have to make outgoing calls, sometimes placing a call for your boss, sometimes making a call yourself in relation to some office matter. You should create a list of your regularly called telephone numbers. This will save time and frustration in having to look up numbers constantly or call Information for a number. Where possible, secure the direct-dialing number, thus saving waiting time while your call is routed through a central switchboard. List these numbers in a card index system, from which cards can be readily entered or discarded. Depending on the nature of your boss's relationship with the person, the individual's name, company, and telephone number are must items; mailing addresses may be useful; other information, such as spouse's name, children's names, special professional or personal interests, may be useful at times if your boss wants to use this kind of information in her dealings with the person. Some bosses like to make a letter or call sound more personal by asking to be remembered to a wife or husband (and if the person's spouse's name is on the index card to remind your boss, she's more likely to use the right name).

When you place a call for your boss, it makes a splendid impression to ask the person you are calling (or his secretary), "Are you (Is Mr. Jones) free to accept a call from Miss Smith at this time?" This accomplishes several things at once: it establishes that Miss Smith is calling; it flatters Mr. Jones in that it assumes he may be too busy right now to take Miss Smith's call; it also flatters him by giving him the choice of taking the call; it allows him time to get papers or documentation together before calling Miss Smith back. Normally, you'll get right through.

The Telephone Power Game

Some executives play a power game on who places calls and who answers the telephone first. Other executives like to receive and place their own calls directly unless they are busy in meetings or have visitors. You will soon learn which is which. The question, "Are you free to accept a call from . . ." tends to blunt the force of the power game by its gentle courtesy.

"Is He In?"

Until you get to be on good speaking terms with an answering secretary, avoid asking, "Is he in?" when the phone is answered. This friendly shortcut works well with frequently made calls when you and the answering secretary are on good terms, but is rude when tried with someone you seldom call.

When placing a call on an office matter, say, "This is (your name), calling for Miss Smith of ABC Company." Then ask for the information you want. This formula quickly identifies who you are, what company you are calling for, and who your boss is. The identification of your boss's name is necessary only when the call is on her behalf and her name is the key to securing the data or action you are seeking. Sometimes you may need to refer to her title or responsibility in the company in order to get the action or response you need. By giving this information, you let the person taking the call know the level of responsibility in your company with which he is dealing.

"I'll Transfer You"

When placing a call to a person with a certain specific responsibility in a large company, you may end up being shunted from one office to another. Keep a scrap-paper listing of the number of transfers; after four or five, feel free to get indignant and to let the next person who answers know that she is now the sixth person you have talked to trying to find out where to find your information. That will tend to focus attention on getting you to the proper party more quickly. And keep this experience in mind when someone is being shunted around in your telephone system; ask for the information required and tell the caller that the right party will call back. Then find out who in your company should make the call and pass the request to that person. To that caller *you* are the ABC Company. Since you know your company better than an outsider does, you should ensure that the right person in your company is located, rather than passing the caller on to a seemingly endless succession of transfers.

Get the Number Right

When you take down telephone numbers, repeat the number to ensure you have it right. It is frustrating to your boss when she is returning a call and the number you gave her is not the right number. In like manner, when you give your number for someone to call back, repeat it yourself if the other person does not repeat it back to you.

Ending a Call

Always close a telephone conversation with a pleasant word. "Have a good day" is trite; so is "Take care." "Thank you so much for your help" is fine; so is "It's such a pleasure to find someone so helpful." Even "Goodbye, Mr. Jones" is excellent, since Mr. Jones has heard his name used in a pleasant manner. If the caller or the person who answers your call hangs up with the feeling of "that was nice," your next call will be welcomed. Even if you are calling about an unpleasant matter, you can convey a personable manner in dealing with it. Such a manner will generally get more accomplished and help to maintain more relationships than will angry confrontation. If confrontation is unavoidable, it is better for your boss to handle the matter.

"Hello"

If you are placing a call and someone answers "Hello," ask if this is the XYZ Company or Mr. Jones's office. By doing that you can quickly make sure you've reached the number you are seeking.

"I'll Put You On Hold"

If you answer a call and need to put the person on hold, ask first if that is satisfactory or whether the person would prefer a call back. Often the caller is phoning from a long distance and does not want to wait on a dead telephone line without even being given an alternative. If the caller is on hold and it begins to look as though your boss will not be able to reach the phone soon, get back to the caller and explain the situation, suggesting that your boss will call back promptly. Sometimes the person on hold has decided not to wait any longer or has had something arise that forces him to hang up. If you know who it is, try to have the call returned as soon as possible. If you don't know who it is, but the person soon places the call again, try to put him through without further waiting.

Managing Voice Mail

"Voice mail" can be easily understood as a computerized answering machine shared by everyone in an office. With voice mail, callers can either leave messages or receive stored information that has been saved on the system. The systems are designed to be easily understood and usually involve following the instructions which are played as you use the system. For example, a caller is instructed to press different numbers to access different areas of the system, to leave messages or to play messages. Usually everyone in the system has a code to insure the privacy of the messages they receive.

Depending on the equipment your office uses, you may be required to manage the system in some way. You may have the power to pick up messages for your boss or to transfer callers into the system after speaking to them first. Used properly, voice mail can reduce the time and effort you spend taking messages from people. So if it is available, use the system whenever possible and be prepared to coach clients and customers in employing voice mail.

Complex Phone Systems

Telephone systems have become more complex and sophisticated at a very rapid pace. Many new developments have been promised by manufacturers and developers. Business, traditionally very dependent on the telephone, will probably become more so with the new features being introduced. You will probably find yourself fulfilling a more sophisticated role in managing the phone system in your office for both yourself and your boss.

Features now available in most areas include call waiting, call holding, conference calling, intercoms, transferring, speed-dial or auto-dial, redial, hold, mute, and speakerphone. Using these phones properly involves some simple programming, but your manual will probably provide you with all the information you need.

One very helpful accessory is a telephone headset. This allows you to speak on the phone while using the computer or handling papers. You probably do this now by pressing your shoulder up toward your ear or using the speakerphone. Headsets allow you to speak privately and clearly and to avoid the chronic back pain that secretaries often develop as a result of improper use of the telephone.

CHAPTER THREE

Reception

Depending on the size and organization of your company, a receptionist may preside over a lobby or reception area to welcome visitors from outside the firm. This receptionist usually serves as an initial screen: securing the visitor's name, company, purpose of visit, person to be visited, and calls you with that information if the person wants to see your boss.

Kinds of Visits

Several conditions are possible:

A Previously Made Appointment

1. The person has made a previous appointment and is expected. The visitor may be an old friend of your boss's or a stranger.

This, then, may be a first visit or one of a long series. Your boss may be free to see the person right on time, or something unexpected may have come up that requires the visitor to wait.

What you do depends on whether your boss is free right away. If he is, simply tell your boss that his expected visitor is in the waiting room and ask whether you should go to get him. If the visitor can be seen at once, let the receptionist know that you are coming to the reception room immediately. If the visitor will have to wait awhile, let the receptionist know about how long that might be. Although a visitor naturally prefers to be ushered in promptly to see the person with whom he has an appointment, it is always courteous—and good for the relationship—to keep him informed about the length of any unexpected wait.

Who goes to greet the visitor depends on who the visitor is and how your boss likes to manage such matters. Normally you will go to the reception room, ask for the visitor by name, identify yourself, and guide the person to the office. You would show him into the office, simply announcing his presence if he's an old friend or introducing him if he's a first-time visitor. If, however, the visitor is a VIP or an old friend (or both), your boss may want to go to the reception room personally to welcome this guest. If that happens, smile and say hello as the two pass your desk. If you already know the person, this renews your personal acquaintance; if this is a new visitor, you may well have occasion to speak to him on the phone in the future and this initial pleasantry makes the future relationship easier for both of you.

In some instances, you may be working in an office with no separate receptionist or waiting room. In this case, you have to combine several functions in quick succession. Ascertain who the visitor is, determine whether the visitor is known to your boss, find out if your boss is free (or willing) to see him, put the visitor at ease while waiting, take any coats that need hanging up, and inform the visitor how long he might have to wait if there is a delay. In such a situation, the waiting area is often close to your desk, so you have to continue with your own work while being watched by the visitor for any clues about when he can see your boss. You need to blend a friendly personableness with an official reserve, so you can do your work without shutting the visitor out as though he were an inconvenience. You never know how important any visitor will be to your company's business, so always try to make his welcome and wait as pleasant as possible. It sometimes helps to put yourself in his position and remember the Golden Rule: treat each visitor with as much thoughtfulness and courtesy as you would like to be shown.

No Previously Made Appointment

2. The visitor does not have an appointment. In such a case, he may be an old friend of your executive who is dropping in on the off chance they can spend a few minutes together. Or the visitor may be a salesperson who is trying to break into your boss's day, hoping to make a sale. Or it could be someone with an idea that could change the nature of your company. The receptionist will give you the initial information that the visitor first makes known. You then have to do some quick investigation and decision-making. What more can you find out about this visitor and what he wants with your boss? Does your boss know him or want to see him? If the visitor is known and your boss does not want to see him, you will have to turn him away with

---

Tip

Your own "company reputation" grows according to how you treat your visitors, and how well you support your boss.

graceful regrets. You may never see him again, but, then again, he may become very important to the company. You may forget him, but he will not forget the manner in which he was denied access to your boss. Again, put yourself in his place. Tell him that your boss is not free to see him today, or that the company already secures services from a vendor with whom it is very happy, and is not considering any change at the present. You might say your boss would very much like to see him at a mutually convenient time, and ask the visitor to please call and confirm an appointment in three weeks. You could explain that your boss likes to see initial proposals in writing before making appointments, and invite the visitor to write a letter summarizing the proposition he wishes your boss to look at before an appointment is scheduled.

If the visitor is someone who has pestered your boss, explain how busy your boss is, that this is not a good time to even say "hello," and is there any message he would like to leave? Even though the person goes away without having accomplished his mission—which was to see your boss—he should go away with the feeling that he has been considered important as an individual, has been listened to, and that his concern will be expressed to your boss. Tact and a touch of diplomacy keep your boss's special place of esteem in the eyes of this kind of visitor while at the same time preserving your boss's time and privacy.

The Visitor Is Early

3. The visitor is early. Not just five minutes early, but thirty-five minutes early. In such a case, your boss may be just as happy to see him and get the appointment over with that much sooner. If that is the situation, the only problem you have is knowing how this change of schedule will affect the succeeding events in your boss's day.

If, however, your boss cannot see the visitor until the appointed time, you may have to suggest a convenient way of filling in some time. If the visitor has work or reading he has brought with him, you won't need to help him fill in the time. Otherwise, you may ask him if he would like to see the latest copy of some magazine (popular, news, or trade) which you have in the office. Or you might get him a copy of the morning newspaper, if one is nearby. Offer him a cup of coffee while he waits. You are not really obligated to do any of these things, since he is the one who arrived early and created the problem. However, by suggesting something to fill in his time, if there are no reading materials in the waiting area, you can be assured he will be most appreciative. And he will probably make some comment to your boss about how helpful you were.

Your Boss Is Running Behind Schedule

4. Your boss is running late and cannot see the visitor for thirty minutes. Now the shoe is on the other foot and you do have an obligation to soothe his feelings. Your boss will apologize when he sees him, but you can offer a kind of peace offering in the form of a cup of coffee and the latest issue of the trade magazine that covers your business. The apology will be more readily accepted and the meeting will not have to overcome the caller's initial barrier of hurt feelings or resentment at being considered secondary to some other demand.

The Visitor Is Late

5. Your visitor is thirty minutes late and rushes, spewing breathless words of frustration at traffic delays. Your boss has a full day of appointments that will be affected in some way by this delay. First, put your visitor at ease and accept his explanation at face value, sympathize with him about the problems of getting about at this hour, and tell him you will let your boss know he has arrived. Allow the visitor a couple of minutes to collect himself after rushing in breathlessly.

You may then suggest—as you usher the visitor toward your boss's office—that your boss has a very full day and you know Mr. Smith will be grateful if the visitor could keep in mind that Mr. Smith's next appointment is in forty-five minutes. By doing this, you have tactfully given the visitor a schedule within which to conduct his business with your boss.

Confirm the Appointment

Some secretaries find it useful to call people who have appointments with their boss the day before the appointment just to confirm that it is still on the visitor's schedule. This practice achieves several things: it reminds the visitor that your boss takes his appointment schedule seriously and is busy enough to need this confirmation; it flatters the visitor that your boss should think so highly of him as to confirm the reservation; it sometimes unearths the fact that the appointment was forgotten (which the visitor would probably not admit to you), that it is no longer possible due to schedule conflicts that have arisen, or no longer needed due to

the changing business situation. The net result is a smoother day for your boss and a pleased business colleague who was called the day before his scheduled appointment. These calls may take fifteen to thirty minutes during the day, but they are well worth the effort if your boss has a tight schedule.

You may choose to limit such calls to people who, you have learned, tend to forget or run late. But interestingly, the ones who appreciate such a call the most are the ones who normally don't need to be called. What they appreciate is being thought of; they also will admire your efficiency.

Who Makes the Appointment

Some people will call to make an appointment with your boss. Some executives make their own appointments; some want you to make routine appointments for them, reserving the option to veto such an appointment. You need to work out with your boss the appointment system he wants to adopt. If you do have the responsibility of making some appointments for him, you should always do so tentatively and tell the person who wants the appointment that you will confirm it after you clear it with your boss. You might suggest that you need to check with his calendar. You can then reschedule the appointment when you confirm it, or cancel it altogether if your boss does not want to see this person.

Keeping the Master Appointment Calendar

Every day, update your appointment calendar with your boss's so that you are both

> **Tip**
> Your role as guardian of the door to your boss's office calls for sensitivity and judgment.

expecting the same people at the same time. If your boss has been running his own appointment-reception service, this may take a little tactful training on your part. But the end result will be a smoother life for him and a much more controlled life for you. The management of his appointment and reception service is an important way you can take a great load off his shoulders, enabling him to give his time and energy to his work instead of trying to control his visitors as well as do his work. You may have to point out all the benefits before he turns this job over to you in full, but once he's done it, he'll never want it back.

Company Visitors

Some visitors are colleagues from other departments in the company. Some will call ahead to make an appointment to see your boss, while others just wander by and want a quick word with him. Depending on the nature of the relationship with your boss—and the person's position in the company—he may feel free to stick his head in your boss's door and interrupt him without giving it a second thought. He might want a short discussion of some problem or to just tell your boss the latest joke making the rounds. Or the person may be a junior executive who stands in some awe of your boss, wants to see him on some matter of importance, or hopes to make a positive

impression and be remembered. This last type of company visitor will more likely go through you to set up an appointment.

Regardless of which kind of company visitor wants to see your boss, you should treat him pleasantly and helpfully. Your own "company reputation" grows according to how you treat your visitors, and how well you support your boss. People in the company will begin to hear about you, often before you actually meet them, and much of what they hear is in comments made by company visitors to your boss.

If your boss is busy or out of his office when a company visitor drops by, be sure to make a note of the visit and any comments regarding the purpose of the visit. The effectiveness of your boss's work in the company is often based on snippets of information about plans, problems, and people that drop his way quite casually. His company visitors are an indispensable source of such bits of information. And part of your job is to help keep the flow of information coming his way by helping company visitors feel at ease when coming to see him. Your boss will let you know which company visitors are to be discouraged.

A Tactful Guardian of the Door

Acting as guardian of the door to your boss's office calls for sensitivity and judgment. Some secretaries are possessive: they think they always know what is best for their boss and strive to protect him from interruptions they don't approve of. They may think they are keeping him from "just another salesman," when, in fact, they may be turning away an invaluable new service or major new idea that would be of great help to the company. People from outside the company accept being turned aside once your boss has heard them enough to grasp what they propose and then explains that the time or the conditions are not right to consider the matter further. They at least have the sense that they received some consideration before being told no. But they will become highly dissatisfied if they feel that a secretary has preempted the boss's role and decided that their proposal will never even be placed before the boss for consideration. Although they would prefer to talk to the boss directly, you will reduce dissatisfaction if you carefully take down the particulars of their proposal, place it before your boss, and later call back to relay his decision not to see them or not to proceed further with the matter. They at least feel that their proposal—in whatever limited form, compared with how they themselves would have presented it—was considered by your boss and not blocked by his secretary.

A Note About Out-of-Town Visitors

Often people who are visiting your city or town for a day or two on business try to set up several appointments during their visit. They will first try to establish the most important ones—those that are already linked with present business and are intended to maintain or increase that business. Once those are scheduled, they will try to build appointments for new prospects around the times already committed. Your boss might be on the "old business" list or the "prospect" list. Both are important to the visitor—and may be important to your boss. Business is built on an ever increasing circle of acquaintances and knowledge of related businesses.

CHAPTER FOUR

Correspondence

Correspondence flows in two directions: from outside your office to your boss and from your boss to those outside your office. Some of the letters your boss writes originate with her; some are part of or develop into an ongoing correspondence for which a large file grows; some are replies to letters sent to her.

Incoming Correspondence

Companies and bosses vary on how incoming mail is handled. Generally the mail is first delivered to a central mail room, where it is sorted by floor and office. During the day someone from the mail room makes two or three deliveries of mail that has accumulated for your office. This mail includes both letters from outside correspondents and interoffice letters and memos.

In some companies all mail addressed to the company is opened in the mail room. If checks or money orders are enclosed, they are separated, accounted for, banked, and their amount and purpose noted. The letters are then sent to the appropriate department for handling. In such a company, your boss's mail and any mail addressed to you or of a nature to be handled by your boss would come to your desk opened. In these companies, envelopes marked "Personal" or "Confidential" would probably arrive on your desk unopened by the mail room.

In most companies, however, mail addressed to the company in general is opened in the mail room, while mail addressed to a particular person is sent directly to that person for opening. In this case, all letters addressed to your boss or you would arrive on your desk unopened. Letters addressed to the company that the mail-room people think are your boss's responsibility to handle would arrive opened.

You and your boss must agree on how she wants you to prepare her mail. First of all, you must determine how to recognize personal mail from business mail. She may receive certain private business mailings at the office that she alone wants to handle. She has to tell you which firms or people might send her personal mail; place those letters on her desk unopened and in their own pile.

She will generally want you to open all her business mail. You both should decide whether mail marked "Personal" or "Confidential" includes you or not. In answering this question, much depends on the nature of the business and your boss's role within the business. You can expect increasingly to be a confidant in most of her business life—with the possible exception of certain personnel matters and possible future reorganizational topics. But even in these, you will become trusted to handle this kind of information in its early stages as your relationship with your boss grows in mutual reliance.

When you have opened the mail, organize it into three or four categories you have agreed upon with your boss. Possible categories are:

1. Urgent: These are letters that require immediate attention. Her response to these letters might be to dictate an answer at once, start an investigation for further in-

formation, or call the person. You will soon learn which letters are really urgent and which are merely important.

If you separate the urgent letters from others, she can at least focus on the former if she has only a short time in the office between meetings or appointments.

2. The important letters she will have to answer herself, but which are less than urgent.

3. The need-to-read-but-no-action-required letters: Much of an executive's career is based on having timely information about her business, company, colleagues, competitors, and trends in her field. Many people will send mailings or copies of correspondence which do not require her personal action, but are part of the context in which she has to work and make decisions.

4. Magazines, journals, newspapers, monographs, and the like: You'll see general-interest magazines and newspapers (*Time* or *The Wall Street Journal*, for instance), trade or professional publications, and technical monographs and books. She may wish to leaf through these for whatever information she can quickly glean, or to study some particular subject in great detail. Your boss can guide you in evaluating the importance she places on the various kinds of printed material that cross your desk.

5. Special reports and studies: From time to time your boss may be on a committee or task force that requires the reading or preparation of special reports or studies. These reports can often be quickly perused, but sometimes call for intensive study prior

to a meeting. Timing and the nature of your boss's connection with the project will determine whether these reports go in her urgent pile or in her "will read, if possible" stack.

Before you place the correspondence on her desk, you can take several steps. These should be discussed with her so you both agree on your actions:

1. Highlight the subject matter or response requested. Use a colored underline or highlighter. This will draw attention at once to the main point of the letter. She can read the rest of it if it is a matter that directly concerns her, or she can decide that it is of only incidental interest and not spend any more time on the letter.

2. Get the file, if this is part of an ongoing correspondence, and send the letter and file in together. This will save having to get it later, and will enable your boss to answer the letter in light of what both parties have said in the past.

3. Use a date stamp and mark the letter when you first process it. It is sometimes more important to know when you received the letter than when the writer dated it.

A Correspondence List

If your boss is away for several days, it is helpful to have her mail especially well-organized when she returns. For instance, all her urgent mail should be in a single folder. Separate folders can be prepared for each day's "important but not urgent" mail, with a short summary of the person, company, and subject matter typed on a sheet attached to the cover of the folder. All of the "to read" mail can be in a single folder, as can printed magazines and newspapers.

By doing this, it will be much easier for her to care for urgent and important correspondence as quickly as needed, while background information and general reading can wait their turn in her schedule.

Marking the Letter

It is useful if you and your boss agree to use a particular color pen or pencil for marking a letter. Your underlining or highlighting or any notes you might make on the letter should always be in the same color. Hers should be in another, consistent color. Many executives merely check a corner in that color to indicate they have seen the letter. If she does this, both of you know that an unmarked letter means an unread letter; this is often a useful fact to know when trying to reconstruct a file or a sequence of actions.

Any notes she makes on the letter asking you to secure more information should be made in "her color" pen or pencil. Any notes you jot down in response should be made in "your color." This practice makes the flow

Tip
    As you grow in familiarity with the job and in your working relationship with your boss, you will be able to handle many matters for her on your own.

> **Tip**
> Many routine matters might, in time, be handled in your name rather than hers. Don't seek this responsibility too quickly, but don't wait indefinitely for your boss to suggest that you handle what you can obviously do perfectly well.

of information very quick and obvious, eliminating time spent trying to figure out who made which notations.

Matters You Can Handle

As you grow in familiarity with the job and in a working relationship with your boss, you will be able to handle many matters on your own, but for her. You can separate these letters, research the matter in the files if necessary, and write an appropriate response for your boss's signature. When you place this before her for signature, you should include the original letter for her to glance over. By doing this, you not only take over a more or less routine task, but you also keep her fully informed so she is never surprised if she meets the writer sometime outside the office and hears about the contents of her letter.

Again, depending on the nature of the business and on your relationship with your boss, many of these routine matters might, in time, be handled in your name rather than hers; incoming correspondence relating to them would begin to be addressed to you. Our advice is, don't reach for this responsibility too quickly, but don't wait indefinitely for your boss to suggest that you handle what you can obviously do perfectly well.

Outgoing Correspondence

Letter writing is a major part of a secretary's job. Many of those letters will originate with your boss. The form they take varies with her work patterns and the size of your company. She may write out a draft letter in longhand. Your job then is to transcribe it on the typewriter or word processor. This method can take her longer than is most efficient for routine letters, but may be the best way for her to think through a complex problem and get it down on paper carefully.

You might type out a first draft of such a letter with double spacing so she can refine it before proceeding to the final single-spaced letter or report. She may type out a draft letter herself—some executives like to have a typewriter handy. After she has refined her own first draft, you then type out the final letter or report.

She may dictate the letter. In the past, all secretaries learned shorthand and executives dictated face-to-face. Even though some system of shorthand or speed writing is useful at times, fewer secretaries learn this skill and fewer executives request it. Electronic dictating systems, some with portable dictating units and others with telephone-dictating access, have just about replaced the direct executive-to-secretary, dictation-by-shorthand method. Indeed, in many larger offices, routine transcription is now handled by a word-processing department that processes overnight the dictation telephoned in by dozens of executives. In such an office, you as a secretary are more likely to manage the flow of dictation between your boss and the word-processing department than to type out the correspondence yourself.

In smaller companies, your boss may have a dictating recorder she can take home or on a trip; you would have a transcribing unit that plays back her dictation tape through earphones or a speaker. Usually you control the playback with foot controls and type out or word-process her correspondence throughout the course of the day.

Your boss may be an expert dictator, or she may need your suggestions on improving her dictation. She should spell out new or unusual names or words, and specify where she wants periods, paragraphs, or any special punctuation or indentation. She should learn to speak crisply—including consonants—and reasonably slowly. You can slow up the transcribing playback if she talks too quickly to understand readily, but that lowers the tone of her voice on the unit. With each tape or disk of dictation, she should return all the correspondence she used when dictating so you have a complete file and can refer to the original correspondence in determining proper names and addresses. Sometimes she'll use a paper tab to mark the length of correspondence—and even note which letters are to be given priority in processing. If she uses this tab system, you should ensure that her unit has a fresh supply of tabs before she takes it on an extensive business trip.

Years ago, secretaries had to type a letter perfectly on a manual typewriter. Since no one can do that constantly, the secretary had to learn how to erase the original with little or no mess—and four or five carbons. This was very time-consuming and inefficient. Today's secretary has a correcting electric typewriter (with either a lift-off correction tape or a cover-over correction tape) and a photocopy machine. The letter can be readily corrected line by line as it is typed, and proofread while it is still in the typewriter. The photocopies are exact replicas of the original corrected final copy; no carbon copies need correcting. A secretary might have an electronic typewriter that holds the letter in memory; if mistakes are detected, they can be easily corrected without disturbing the rest of the text and a corrected final copy can be quickly run off. Increasingly, more secretaries have word-processing systems that combine a display screen with a large memory. Here, too, corrections can be readily made, and corrected final copies run off. In market studies of the early 1980s, one major office-machine corporation found it sold nine correcting electric typewriters for every one electronic typewriter and ten electronic typewriters to every word processor, but the ratio changes each year in favor of electronic typewriters and word processors.

The spectre of the perfect letter—and perfect carbons—does not present the problems it once did before the advent of the electronic office. Most word-processing programs even have spelling checks that can locate obvious typographical errors. These spelling checks do not pick up words that are spelled correctly but are the wrong words, such as "than" for "that" or "is" for "in." You still have to proof your letter for sense, even though your word-processing spelling check has found all your *tehs* and *fos*.

Business letters today are usually typed flush left—every line begins at the left-hand margin. A minimum of punctuation appears at the end of lines. The reason for this goes beyond clean appearance; it is based on time and motion studies that focused on using the least number of keystrokes. Because each keystroke takes a fraction of a second and makes possible the introduction of another error, fewer keystrokes mean less time spent in typing and correcting a letter—hence, less cost in the overall preparation of the letter. For one or two letters, this may not seem to add up to much of a saving, but when multiplied by many thousands of letters over the years, the savings are substantial. A standard flush-left letter has the following characteristics:

Date

The date is normally expressed as *December 12, 1999* with no punctuation other than the comma between the day and the year. In the military and many government offices, and increasingly in many corporations, the date is expressed as *12 December 1999* (as it is in most European countries) with no punctuation at all. In both cases, the month is fully spelled out. Abbreviations for months are considered informal and not suitable for business correspondence. In some offices and in many govern-

ment agencies that use documents in scanned computer applications, the date is expressed in numbers only in the sequence of year-month-day, with all months and days expressed in two-digit figures. The computer can then sort dates easily. In this system, *January 1, 1999* is expressed as *19990101; December 25, 1999* is *19991225*. In a computer sort of these numbers, the earlier and later dates are easily put into chronological order; this is much more difficult for a computer to do when dates are expressed in the more standard ways.

Name, Title, Company, Address, City

The first line of the formal address is the name of the person to whom the letter is being sent. You may use the title of address, such as *Mr., Mrs., Miss,* or *Ms.* In some instances, you would use a title that is related to a position or profession, such as *Senator, Congressman, The Rev.,* or *The Hon.* Increasingly, however, these titles of address are not included in business letters. Here again, keystrokes are saved; and the awkward decision of how to address a woman is postponed until the opening salutation.

When the person's company title is used, it is usually placed on the first line, separated from the person's name by a comma: Janice L. Resnick, President, or William T. Smith, Production Manager.

The second line is usually the company name, spelled out in full or with commonly

---

Tip
Keep an index file for people and firms with whom you regularly correspond, and list their zip codes in the file.

advertised abbreviations. Abbreviations for businesses are considered an alternate (or sometimes primary) legal name for the company. Both *International Business Machines Corporation* and *IBM Corporation* are acceptable. In the interest of saving keystrokes, the abbreviations that are in common use without any periods should be typed accordingly (*IBM,* not *I.B.M.*).

The third line is the street address or box number. If there is a special floor or department, it is often used as the fourth line.

The fourth line is the city, state, and zip. With the post office steadily proceeding toward optical scanning of addresses for sorting purposes, the two-letter post office abbreviations for the state are in general use: MA, not Mass., CT, not Conn., CA, not Calif., and NY, not N.Y. Here again, keystrokes are saved. You will soon learn the abbreviations for states you commonly send letters to, but you will need to keep a list of all fifty states in your desk for the times you send a letter to a state whose abbreviation has slipped your mind. You can obtain a list from the company mail room or the post office.

A fifth line may be used for another country.

The postal service wants all mail to have zip codes. It will not accept bulk or Express Mail unless the zip code is part of the address. Normally you will be corresponding regularly with people, so their zip code is available to you from their correspondence. If you have much correspondence without such information, you should get a postal zip code information book (through your purchasing department). This look lists every zip code in the country, with street numbers in cities and towns that have more than one zip code.

Keep an index file for people and firms with whom you regularly correspond, and include their zip codes in the file.

Salutation

The opening word of greeting is called a salutation. In business correspondence it usually consists of the word *Dear* followed by the person's name: Dear Bill, Dear Mr. Smith, Dear Ms. Adams, or Dear Senator Brown. If you know a woman to be married or single, the appropriate *Mrs.* or *Miss* is acceptable, although many businesswomen increasingly prefer *Ms.* as a counterpart to the masculine *Mr.* The salutation is followed by a colon in business correspondence and by a comma in informal correspondence.

Addressing a firm presents a further problem. Once *Dear Sir:* was standard, with *Dear Sir/Madam:* used occasionally. Often the single word *Gentlemen:* was employed. Today, with business-letter writers as well as book writers trying to avoid sexist language, the easiest way to address a firm is to use the firm's name: Dear RCA: or Dear Wagner & McCready. People at the firm will route the letter to the proper person to deal with your letter, regardless of the salutation you used.

On your index cards for correspondence, note how your boss likes to address a person. Some are *Mr. Jones;* some are *Bob* when the formal name is *Robert,* but some *Roberts* are called *Robert.* And some *Roberts* might even be *Bud* or some other nickname unrelated to their formal name. Use the formal name in the address and the more personal name in the salutation. Get your boss into the habit of mentioning which salutation she prefers when she dictates her

> **Tip**
>   The language used in business correspondence is concrete, direct, to the point. It does not try to create literary effects or to use much humor or wit. It is writing for the sake of conveying clear, unambiguous communication; it is not intended to be beautiful or memorable writing.

letters. If she gives you a list of names and addresses for letters with identical contents to process, ask her to note how she wants the salutation for each letter.

Body of the Letter

Each paragraph of the letter starts with the first word flush to the left-hand margin. Paragraphs are separated by a line of space. It is generally good practice to restrict a letter to a single topic of business, for several reasons: if the person receiving a multitopic letter handles one of the topics, she may file the letter before addressing the other topics; it is difficult to know where to file a multitopic letter; cross-referencing such a letter in a filing system is costly and often unreliable. If your boss has five items she wants to write someone about, it is better to write five short letters—one on each point—than to write one long letter covering all five points.

Each letter should normally begin with an opening paragraph, which includes reference to earlier correspondence or telephone calls, indicating the subject about which the letter is being written. The next paragraph or two should develop that subject, specifying any action that is needed or has taken place. The final paragraph should conclude with any request or promise of future action or information.

Conclusion

Many business-letter writers close a letter with a standard phrase of conclusion, such as *With every good wish*, or *With all kind regards*. This is a polite way of concluding a letter without seeming to close it abruptly and rudely. A comma normally follows this line; if your boss adds the words *I am (With every good wish, I am)* or *I remain* to the phrase, no punctuation follows the phrase.

Complimentary Closing

This formal closing of the letter usually consists of *Sincerely, Sincerely yours*, or *Best wishes*, in business letters. *Truly yours*, and *Very truly yours*, seem to have passed out of general use. This line, too, is followed by a comma.

Name

Leave about five lines for the signature and then type the full name. Many signatures are so stylized (a polite way of suggesting they're often illegible) that it is a service to the recipient to be able to see the name typed out. Five lines gives plenty of space for a large, flowing signature, yet a small, tight one is equally enhanced by the surrounding spaciousness.

If your boss uses letterhead with her name and title printed on the stationery, you won't need to type her title after her name below the signature since that information is already provided. Indeed, some executives do not want their name typed after the signature, feeling that it is not needed since the name is printed. If, however, your boss uses general company stationery, both her name and title should be typed. The name line has no concluding punctuation, nor does the title line.

If you write a letter in your own name, you should normally use your boss's letterhead and write *Secretary to Miss Smith* after your own name on the name line.

Dictator/Secretary

It is normal to include the initials of the dictator and secretary. Sometimes only the initials of the secretary are typed, since the dictator's name is on the letter. If the dictator's initials are *JDS* and the secretary's *MFB*, the pattern might be *JDS/mfb*, *JDS:MFB*, or simply *mfb*. This notation is placed at the left margin of the letter, four or five lines after the typed name of the sender.

Copies and Enclosures

It is normal to indicate to whom copies are sent and to list any enclosures. Once the abbreviation *CC* or *cc* was used for "carbon copies." This abbreviation is still in use, even though the copies are more likely to be photocopies. Increasingly, the word *Copies* is used, followed by a colon and the list of people receiving copies in alphabetical order. On each copy, you would normally draw an arrow pointing to the name of the person that copy was going to. Enclosures are indicated by *Encl* followed by a colon and the items enclosed.

The list of people to whom copies were sent is useful both to your boss and to those who receive the copies. Your boss will have a record for the future of who was sent a copy of the letter. Each one who receives a copy will know who else has the information contained in the letter. Sometimes a "blind copy" is sent to someone for special reasons. That person's name is not listed on the "Copies" list, but is listed as a *Blind copy* on your file copy and on the recipient's copy but not on the original. Your boss will thus know she sent a blind copy, and the person receiving the copy will know that others are unaware he has the information.

Enclosures are listed for two reasons: you will know from your file copy what other material was included in the original mailing; the person receiving the mailing will know if anything he was supposed to have received was inadvertently left out.

Tip
   Work should go to your boss as perfect as you can make it. Never try to slip away from this responsibility by saying, "It was their fault."

A standard business letter will look like this:

March 28, 1999

Richard C. Brown, DP Manager
ABC Company, Inc.
123 Fourth Street
Des Moines, IA 45678

Dear Mr. Brown:

I am writing about our telephone conversation this morning, regarding a Destruct-All shredder.

We would be pleased to provide you with a demonstration shredder for two weeks' use with no obligation. You can test its effectiveness and thoroughness in your actual working situation.

Mr. Robert B. Tompkins, our Midwestern representative, will call you early next week to set up a convenient time to install the demonstration model and to review our sales terms. If you decide to purchase a Destruct-All shredder, we can deliver your new shredder at the same time we pick up the demonstrator.

Thank you for turning to us. With every hope we can be of complete service to you, I remain,

Sincerely yours,

John D. Smith
Sales Manager

mfb

Copy: Robert B. Tompkins
Encl: Destruct-All booklet

The language used in business correspondence is concrete, direct, to the point. It does not try to create literary effects or to use much humor or wit. It is writing for the sake of clear, unambiguous communication—often with a stranger; it is not intended to be beautiful or memorable writing. It tends to be more impersonal than personal, more correct than idiomatic, more formal than informal, friendly but businesslike.

Sometimes your boss will add a personal paragraph at the close of a business letter to deepen a personal relationship or friendship that has grown out of the business relationship. In fact, a level of relationship can develop in which a business letter would be considered rude and even hostile by the receiver if those personal notes were missing. In such letters, your boss may use more direct language—less stilted business-type language—than she would in a letter to a stranger.

Such a letter might look like this:

December 2, 1999

Robert S. Williams
XUY Company
987 Sixth Avenue
Atlanta, GA 34567

Dear Rob:

I think it's time to come up with a new focus in our advertising campaign. We're increasingly disappointed with the number of orders and dollar amounts drawn from the ads In the trade journals.

Perhaps we need to zero in on more narrowly targeted markets, rather than to wager so much on general corporate promotion. Think through our products and the specific markets that they appeal to. Can you come up with some suggestions of who make up specific demographically identifiable markets of at least 250,000 people by the time we have our next regular meeting in March?

We're depending on you for a breakthrough in this.

Give my warmest regards to Meg, and remind her that we all have a date at the top of Peachtree on me since I lost that bet on the Falcons.

As always,

Sincerely,

John D. Smith

Handwritten Correspondence

Sometimes in the interest of saving time and typing costs, a boss might respond to an inquiry with a handwritten note. This note might be written on the sender's original letter, which is returned to him as his answer. You keep a photocopy, of course, for your record. Another method is to use a memo pad that has carbons or noncarbon copies as a part of the pad. In this method, you send the original and keep a copy for your files. Usually this approach is used when the message is short, the topic is transient (of short-range importance), speed is important, and the person is known to your boss.

Studies show a typewritten business letter costs over eight dollars to produce. This includes such factors as your boss's time; your time, machine costs, postage, and stationery. Little wonder, then, that some bosses will dash off a handwritten note from time to time.

Presentation for Signature

If you type or word-process the correspondence yourself, be sure to proof it carefully before sending it in for signature. Watch especially for dropped words, and for easy-to-make but hard-to-detect errors like "in" where you should have "is." If you have an electronic typewriter or word processor, be sure not to erase the letter until you have proofed it, run out the final copy, and had your boss sign it. It's always possible she will make some minor alteration at the last minute.

When she has an urgent letter to send out by some express-mail method, take the letter in to her to sign as soon as you have completed it. Otherwise, take batches of letters in for signature two or three times a day.

A safe and systematic method is to place the letter—signature page on top if the letter runs more than a single page—in the flap of the envelope. When you pick up the signed correspondence, you need only insure that the letter is signed and that the right envelope is used for the letter. Everything is right there for you to fold and place in the outgoing mail tray or mailbox.

Once you have your boss sign the letter—thus making sure there are no last-minute changes—the copy goes into the file for possible future reference.

If you assign your boss's correspondence to a typing pool or a word-processing department, be sure to proof it before sending it in for her signature. Even though someone else has proofed it earlier, that person may not know just how a certain word is spelled, may mistype a name, or may simply have missed an error. All work should go to your boss as perfect as you can make it. Don't try to slip away from this responsibility by saying, "It was their fault." If you become known by the word-processing de-

---

Tip

Your letter is all the recipient may ever see of your company, your boss, or yourself—so make sure you send a first-class and accurate picture.

partment as a stickler for perfection, they will accept the fact that you are doing your job well and will proof all the more carefully any work they do for you.

Accuracy

When typing a business letter—whether for your boss or for yourself on her behalf—check and double-check for accuracy. Be especially careful about:

Names: No one likes to see his or her name misspelled.

Addresses: Company names and zip codes need close attention.

Figures: It is so easy to transpose numbers or to leave out a decimal point.

Dates: In calling a meeting or reporting on one, it is important to get dates and times correct. Double-check days and dates. For instance, if you use *Friday, March 12, 1999*, check to make sure that the Friday you refer to is indeed March 12. If you miss on either the day or date—for example, if Thursday is really March 12—the reader might show up on the wrong day.

General spelling: If you have any doubt, look it up. It is quicker to use a speller-divider book than a dictionary. Excellent speller-dividers are easily available in bookstores and office-supply stores.

Hyphenation: If you use hyphenation to avoid very short lines in a letter, check the right place to break the word, again using a speller-divider or dictionary. American-style hyphenation is based on how the word is pronounced, whereas British-style hyphenation is based on the roots of the word. The American system hyphenates "democracy" after the first *c:* democ-racy; the British system follows the pattern of hyphenating according to derivation: *demos* (the common people) + *cracy* (rule by), hence the hyphenation demo-cracy. Your American-produced dictionary and speller-divider follow the American usage, but don't think your British correspondents are uninformed if they hyphenate slightly differently.

The problem of just where to hyphenate can get especially tricky when you use a word in different forms. For instance, "philosopher" is hyphenated as phi-los-o-pher, but "philosophic" is philo-soph-ic—all because the accent has shifted. Likewise, the verb "present" is hyphenated pre-sent; the noun "present" is pres-ent. If you have the least question in your mind, look it up.

Your letter is all the recipient may ever see of your company, your boss, or yourself—so make sure you send a first-class and accurate picture.

Usage changes steadily, so do not depend on patterns you learned years ago. And refer to recently published usage books, rather than earlier—and now outdated—editions. Not only do you want to be regarded as accurate, but you also do not want to be considered old-fashioned. For instance, a growing trend is to use fewer and fewer commas in correspondence. "Correct" style is based on thoughtful application of present usage more than on mechanical obedience to certain rules.

In the past the following sentence would have been punctuated this way:

In 1990, the stockholders met in Chicago, Illinois, on March 17. This year, they will meet in the same city and on the same date, too.

Today these sentences are more likely to be typed:

In 1990 the stockholders met in Chicago, Illinois, on March 17. This year they will meet in the same city and on the same date, too.

The overall appearance is cleaner, and meaning is not confused when the commas are left out. If, however, confusion might result without a comma, by all means put it in.

A current set of the following books by your desk will let you solve most questions of accuracy and usage that may arise:

a college-level dictionary (better than a
    short paperback version)
a speller-divider
a usage and style manual
an almanac
a concise encyclopedia

CHAPTER FIVE

The Facsimile (Fax) Machine

Recent legislation for some states dictates important aspects for fax use which are really matters of common sense. You may want to consult with your company's attorney for the laws that apply where you work. Other aspects of fax use are based on common business practice applied to this new technology.

Fax Etiquette

Keep these basic guidelines in mind:

1. Don't send a lengthy fax without notifying the party receiving it.

2. A long fax (over five pages) ties up the machine and may make it impossible for other, more important communications to get through. Try to schedule outgoing faxes to take this into account.

3. When faxing overseas or to other time zones, calculate when the other office is open or closed and when your information will be used.

4. If possible, send nonpriority faxes after 5 P.M. Some machines have an automatic delayed transmission function just for this purpose.

5. Don't be a "fax potato." Some secretaries send faxes to friends in nearby departments in their own company (occasionally not related to the firm's business) and to take-out restaurants. This is misusing the machine, and if you are caught, your manager may not be pleased.

6. Don't use a fax transmission as your

initial means of contact. Send a letter or call first to be sure that sending a fax is acceptable to the recipient.

7. Keep a list of frequently used fax numbers handy for easy reference. You may even want to keep fax numbers with other important phone numbers on your desk. (Both AT&T and NYNEX publish national fax directories; if your company is interested, call your local telephone exchange for more information.)

Keeping Logs of Documents

Many offices keep logs of faxes sent and received. These logs document when a fax was sent or received for accounting purposes, to bill clients or verify the telephone bill, and to create a "paper trail"—a record of the business's correspondence. While logs may vary in different industries, the basic categories include: Date, Time, Number (a chronological number assigned to the document which may also be labeled on the document itself), Recipient, and Project or Client Name.

Learning Your Own Firm's Procedures

Your firm will no doubt have its own specific procedure for sending and receiving faxes. Many firms have fax machines in the mail room; secretaries bring the document with a prepared cover sheet and leave it for the mail-room personnel to send. When a fax arrives, it is delivered from the mail room to the individual. In other firms, individuals or departments may have their own fax machines, which the secretaries use and sometimes share. Some firms have both and the importance or priority of the document determines how the fax is sent. If this is the case, always check with your manager to see how the fax is to be transmitted.

Ask other secretaries or mail-room personnel to show you the firm's procedures and how to fill out any required forms and cover sheets.

How the Fax Machine Works

Your fax machine came with a manual. This is probably the easiest, fastest, and most reliable way to learn how to use your fax machine. Different models have different features, functions, and keyboards, so the manual that came with the model you have will provide the most accurate instruction. If the manual is missing, request a new one from the dealer or manufacturer.

The dealer or sales representative who sold the machine will probably be willing and able to answer any questions you may have. Many dealers also offer a brief training session with the installation of a new machine. Take advantage of this offer. If you missed the training, contact the dealer and request another session.

Most businesses cover their fax machines with a service contract. The service people who maintain and repair the machines can also demonstrate how to use them properly.

Monitoring Fax Paper Supply

Fax paper requires special care in order to be useful. Follow the instructions that come with your paper. This usually includes storage in a cool, dark place. Fax paper is quite expensive and does not store very well after about one year. So order it in the correct quantities and care for it after it is delivered.

When you are reaching the end of a roll, the paper that comes out is very curly. You may also notice a red or pink mark on the back of the paper which indicates the roll is almost finished. This curly paper is difficult to work with, as it doesn't lie flat. You may wish to remove the roll before it gets to this point, although it will mean wasting some of the paper.

It is a good idea to periodically open the machine and check the paper supply, especially when you know that you will be receiving a long fax, or on Friday afternoons, in case several documents are received when the office is closed.

Keeping Machine On or Off

Most firms leave the fax machine on twenty-four hours a day. This is especially important if your business communicates with people who work late or are in different time zones. Fax machines cater to an information-hungry business environment. To turn off the fax machine would basically defeat the purpose of having one.

Junk Fax

Sometimes you may receive what has become known as "junk fax" or faxes that you do not want to receive. These are usually sales material and advertisements. You will want to stop these faxes as quickly as possible if you receive them. They are expensive for your firm and tie up the machine. Sometimes you can end the transmission by hanging up or disconnecting the caller.

You can request, in writing, that the sender stop transmitting faxes and they will usually stop. If they continue, file a formal complaint with the Better Business Bureau, local Chamber of Commerce, or any agencies governing the industry. Also check with your firm's lawyer, as unsolicited faxes are illegal in some areas.

CHAPTER SIX

Reservations

Sometimes business associates will visit your company for an extended visit, a two- or three-day meeting, or as a party on tour. Your boss may have the responsibility of serving as their official host. As part of that task, arrangements have to be made for travel, dining, hotels, meetings, and sometimes entertainment. Or your boss may have an extended trip for which travel and hotel arrangements need to be made.

One facet of your job is to organize all the arrangements initially and then make last-minute changes as people arrive unexpectedly, fail to arrive, or change their minds at the last moment.

Travel

Today most business people travel by air. If you handle a great deal of air travel, you should encourage your boss to subscribe to the *Official Airlines Guide (OAG)*. It has both North American and International editions. These guides list all scheduled flights by all airlines, together with connecting flights where more than one plane or airline has to be taken from point to point.

If you depend solely on an airline-reservation system for information, you might not get the best deal, as they tend to favor their own system, even though some other airline might offer more convenient flight times or routes and lower prices. Your ability to find your way around the *OAG* will at least enable you to ask good questions about alternative flights and routes.

If you depend solely on a travel agent, you will usually get excellent service. Each agency is tied in with one of the major airline reservation systems for its up-to-the-minute information. Your agent is generally better prepared to know the state of the business, so he, too, can ask the right questions about alternative flights and routes, and especially better prices. However, it doesn't hurt if the agent knows you are reasonably knowledgeable and are looking at alternatives. It will help keep him alert to the very best arrangement for you. When an agent takes your request for granted, he might present the first solution that comes to his computer screen without exploring further.

Since airline deregulation came into effect, pricing has become competitive. (In the past, the Federal Aviation Administration set the fare structure for every route; airlines had to compete in the area of services and style since fares were standard.) Now that fares are flexible, prices for a particular flight can change almost daily. And several different prices exist for seats on the same plane. Even travel agents cannot keep up with all the available rates and the constant changes in rates. You have to ask the agent to find you the best rate available; he, in turn, has to get that information from the airlines on a need-to-know basis.

After deregulation, new airlines quickly came into being. Many were acquired by larger, older airlines before 1990. Most travel agents will think first of the more established airlines they have long been familiar with. Ask them about these newer lines from time to time. To find out which airlines serve your community, glance through ads in the travel or business section of your local newspaper.

If your boss and his associates do a great deal of travel, investigate special travel clubs that will send listings of current air-travel bargains. These clubs usually have a toll-free telephone number and will serve as a travel agent. Although their annual mem-

bership fees are expensive, they specialize in finding seats for their members at the best available rates. In some instances, they may even recommend buying a through-ticket but getting off at an intermediate stop. For instance, your boss may want to travel from Philadelphia to Fort Worth. A Philadelphia–Los Angeles ticket with a change of planes at the Dallas/Fort Worth airport might be several hundred dollars cheaper than a direct Philadelphia–Dallas/Fort Worth ticket. So your boss would buy a Philadelphia–Los Angeles ticket and merely deplane at Dallas/Fort Worth, not using his Dallas/Fort Worth–Los Angeles segment. The only thing to bear in mind for such a flight is the necessity of taking only carry-on luggage; he could not check his luggage only to Dallas/Fort Worth under normal circumstances. That special Philadelphia–Los Angeles via Dallas/Fort Worth rate may be operable only for a three-week period and only on certain days of the week. You could spend hours trying to find this information; your travel agent would probably not be aware of it; the airline would not suggest this possibility; only a travel club committed to searching out such possibilities in the ever changing rate picture would know. Advertisements about such clubs appear in airlines' in-flight magazines, in travel magazines and periodicals for frequent flyers.

The easiest way to purchase tickets once you have determined which flight is best—or have presented the options to your boss and gotten his decision—is to have an account with a local travel agent. The agency will prepare the tickets, deliver them to your office in time for the flight, and bill your company. An alternative is for your boss to use a standard credit card, pick up the tickets at the counter on the day of his flight, and put the bill on his expense account. Given sufficient advance booking time, an airline will mail tickets charged over the telephone to your boss's credit card. The disadvantage of his picking the tickets up at the counter just before the flight is a possible shortage of time. He may be running late in getting to the airport, so a long line for ticketing would be aggravating and could cause him to miss his flight. All too often the person just in front has a long, complex flight schedule to consider, with an equally complex ticket to write up, while the minutes tick by. A late arrival can also result in getting a poor seat, because the better seats may have already been assigned to other passengers.

Many airlines permit advance seat reservations and will also send advance boarding passes. With these in hand, your boss need only present his ticket at the boarding gate, check any luggage with the redcap at the curb, and board the plane. These advance seat reservations and boarding passes are possible for both legs of a round-trip flight. (Smaller airlines tend not to provide these services.)

Reconfirmation

If you have visitors from overseas, their flights will have to be reconfirmed at least seventy-two hours before they are scheduled. Reconfirmation is not always required for flights that originate and terminate in North America. But for any ticket purchased abroad, reconfirmation must be made on all flights that originate in North America, whether they are bound for another North American destination or for an overseas destination. Ask your overseas visitors for their tickets (often two or three books of tickets stapled together). Have them tell you whether they want to make a flight change or will stay with their plans as ticketed. Then call the airline for the next flight at least seventy-two hours prior to that flight and tell them that your visitor is still planning to take the flight as ticketed.

If changes are to be made, the best place to call to take care of them is an office of the airline that first issued the ticket. The next best place is the airline the visitor wants to fly on next.

For a group of visitors, your travel agent might be willing to take all the information—and the tickets—from you and make all the needed changes and reconfirmations for you. However, you should burden your travel agent with this chore only if your overall travel purchases warrant such an imposition on his time and equipment.

As much as possible, find out from your visitors where in the aircraft they like to sit, including smoking or nonsmoking areas. Without promising any results, tell them you'll try to see that the airline accommodates their desires.

VIP Airline Clubs

Most major airlines have private clubs for VIPs. In the early days of commercial flight, membership in these clubs was by invitation only. In recent years, membership is by payment, with only a few airlines retaining the idea of membership by special invitation. Membership can be annual or, for a larger fee, lifetime. It usually includes membership privileges for a spouse. The airline club issues membership cards, which have to be presented at the club for admission.

> **Tip**
>
> Many airlines permit advance seat reservations and will also send advance boarding passes. With these in hand, your boss need only present his ticket at the boarding gate, check any luggage at the curb, and board the plane.

The club provides a quiet, well-appointed place to wait for departure. A receptionist will handle seat reservations and any last-minute travel needs (apart from actual ticketing). Free coffee and tea are available, sometimes free fruit juice and breakfast rolls, and free local telephones. Depending on the airline, a bar may be free or may charge a small amount for drinks. Some clubs offer a small conference room for business meetings.

If he travels constantly, your boss may have an airline VIP club membership paid by the company as a benefit, or he may wish to join one or more on his own. For members of these clubs, a private reservation number is usually provided, and all travel-reservation requests handled through these special numbers receive immediate attention.

Frequent-Flyer Programs

Many major airlines have a special promotion program for frequent flyers. If your boss has reason to travel often on the same airlines, he might well join these frequent-flyer programs. He will be issued a card and a frequent-flyer number. Whenever reservations are made on that airline, give the frequent-flyer number to the airline's reservation representative. This means your boss will be credited with mileage for the flight when he completes it. On some flights, bonus mileage is given at certain times.

Numerous benefits are available for him to select from as he reaches various mileage levels. These include free upgrading to first class, free car rentals, free hotel rooms, free flights, and the like.

Sometimes the frequent-flyer program also has a special reservation number.

Meals

Your visitors may have special food requests. Some may want a kosher meal, others a vegetarian meal, and a third group a salt-free meal. Although it's not widely advertised by the airlines, they will make every effort to provide a passenger with special meals, if given enough advance notice.

When you get preliminary flight information from your visitors, always include a question about any special diet wishes. If they have any, you can let the airline know at the same time you make the reservation or the reconfirmation.

Rental Cars

Ask your boss whether he uses one of the "big three"—Hertz, Avis, or National, or one of the smaller, sometimes less expensive rental agencies. Your company may have an account with one of the companies. If that is the case, your company probably gets a discount on each rental. Your company probably has a policy on whether full insurance is to be taken out each time a car is rented, whether such insurance is covered by a company insurance policy, or whether the company self-insures such coverage. Information about the type of car desired, your boss's driver's-license number, insurance preferences, and discount percentages are fed into a central computer if your boss holds a car-rental frequent-user card or credit card.

Car-rental reservations should be made at the same time as flight reservations. If you use the car-rental frequent-user number or credit card number, the filled-out forms will be waiting for your boss when he arrives at the airport. Otherwise, he will have to wait for a reservations representative at the counter to fill out all the information. Each major car-rental company has a toll-free phone number for making reservations.

Hotels

Your boss may have favorite hotels in different cities he visits on business. He will certainly let you know which these are and ask you to make reservations there when he goes to a particular city. Or he may have favorite hotel systems he uses when possible. If he stays regularly at hotels that are part of a national or international system, call the system to see if they have a hotel in the city he is to visit. If so, make the reservation. If not, check with his second-choice hotel group.

When you make a reservation, call the hotel directly if it is an independent, or use a toll-free number if it is part of a large system. Reservations are normally held until 6 P.M. If your boss may arrive after 6 P.M., you will have to guarantee payment. This is normally done by giving the hotel his credit-card number. When payment is guaranteed, the hotel will hold his room overnight and charge his credit-card account even if he fails to arrive. If payment has been guaranteed at a hotel and his travel plans have changed, be sure to call the hotel to cancel the reservation prior to 6 P.M. of the scheduled arrival day.

Several hotel systems have frequent-traveler programs. Cards and numbers are issued; sometimes a slightly higher fee is charged for "tower suites" reserved for club members. Often rooms are upgraded at no extra cost, and local newspapers are delivered to the room without charge. If your boss is a member of such a program, make his reservations through the special-reservations number when he heads for one of their hotels.

Restaurants

Your boss may have to entertain a dozen visitors who are attending a meeting at your company over a three-day period. He may decide to throw a party for them one evening at a fine local restaurant, and you would make the arrangements.

First, decide with him where the party is to be held. Then call the restaurant and ask to talk with the manager or owner, depending on the size and nature of the establishment. (At some well-known restaurants and hotels, drink and/or meal preparations are handled by a *banquet manager*). Explain that Mr. Smith is entertaining guests and wants them to have an outstanding time. Therefore he has chosen the Bon Appetit Restaurant. You might need to go to the restaurant and choose with the manager an appropriate table and the right menu and wine. Set up an appointment for the visit.

Select a quiet corner—far from the kitchen, the entrance, and the bus stands—where tables can be put together to accommodate the party. If possible, meet the waiter or waitress who will handle the meal and express your appreciation for all the care you know your party will receive.

You may be able to select the menu yourself, depending on how well you know the restaurant, its offerings, and your party. Or you may wish to take a copy of the menu to your boss, with the recommendations of the manager. Are all the meals to be the same? Or is each person to order separately? Much depends on how quickly the party is to be served, and on whether some further activity follows the meal. Seek the manager's advice about the chef's specialties for such a group, even though it may not be listed on the menu. And make arrangements about paying the check, including all tips. Payment could be made with your boss's credit card, by company check, or by billing the company directly. Small restaurants will want payment on the day of the meal, since they have to keep tight control of their cash flow; larger restaurants may be quite pleased to bill your company, hoping for more business in the future. You'll have few problems with a restaurant where your company regularly does business.

Inform your guests that the meal is at a certain time, say 7 P.M. Plan with the manager to start serving at about 7:30 P.M. This will give latecomers time to settle in. People can have drinks while arriving and relaxing. If all your guests are staying at the same hotel, and the restaurant is some distance away, you may have to arrange with the hotel manager or concierge for taxis to deliver them and pick them up. If your guests plan to arrive at the restaurant from various locations, be sure to give them clear directions, including the restaurant's telephone number on a typed card or piece of paper. When you are at the restaurant making preliminary arrangements, you might pick up enough of the restaurant's business cards or matchbooks for each of your guests. Having the card or the matchbook will at least refresh their memory on where they are to be or enable them to have a taxi take them there.

If an event follows the meal, be sure to tell the restaurant manager so he can insure the meal is finished at the proper time. Here again, you may have to make taxi or car-service arrangements to transport your group from the restaurant to the office, the hotel, the theater, or wherever the event is held.

If it is winter and overcoats need checking, it is easier to make arrangements for the coatroom attendant to handle the coats as a group—with payment to be made as part of the restaurant's total bill—than for each guest to deal individually with the coatroom attendant.

If you take part in the meal, quietly keep track of time and services and bring your needs to the manager's attention when necessary. The more successfully you have preplanned and arranged for the party, the less noticed your stage-managing will be. Even though you get involved in conversation with one or more of the guests, keep one eye and ear on how things are going, trying to anticipate any problem in time to mention your concern to the manager. On the other hand, if you do not attend the meal, go over all the arrangements you have made with your boss. Give him a short list of all the details so he will know what you have done and what to expect.

A Small Business Lunch

Your boss may frequently ask you to call a nearby restaurant to make lunch reservations for an office visitor and himself. He may specify the restaurant, or ask you to find a free table at the last moment in one of three or four restaurants he normally patronizes. If he is well-known at the restaurant, getting a good table is easy. Your reservation request goes something like this: "Mr. Smith has an unexpected and important visitor he'd like to take to lunch at Antoine's. Can he get a quiet corner table in half an hour?" When Mr. Smith arrives, he will be greeted by name and cared for at once; his guest will be suitably impressed.

If you are calling a restaurant where Mr. Smith is not known, your reservation request may go something like that: "I am calling for Mr. Smith of ABC Company. He has an unexpected and important visitor that he wants to take special care of. That's why I'm calling Antoine's. Can he have a quiet corner table in half an hour?" Since Mr. Smith is not a regular there, he may not get the corner table, but he'll get the best available table—and again his name will be recognized.

Sometimes your boss may ask you to take a visitor to lunch since he is not available to do so but wants to extend this courtesy to the visitor. Unless you are also known at the restaurant, it may be best to make the reservation in your boss's name, indicating that you are bringing one of his special visitors to lunch. You will probably be expected to pick up the check. Use your boss's account or his credit card, or make arrangements to get enough petty cash before you leave. Get a receipt, including tip, so you can make the required report to the accounting department. Ask your boss to give you clues about what the visitor enjoys talking about. Follow those clues by asking questions and listening with care to learn something new. Every talker knows when he has a good listener. And listening carefully to your boss's visitors is always far safer than talking about him and the company.

Entertainment

From time to time your boss may want to provide entertainment for his out-of-town visitors: theater, concerts, sporting events, and other special activities. The company may have several season tickets, for instance, to home games of a local professional or college team. If so, he might prefer to give the tickets personally to his visitor. Your boss may or may not go with his guest. You may be asked to have the tickets delivered to the visitor's hotel with instructions on how to get to the stadium or arena.

Or you may be asked to make reservations and get tickets for some event in town. You can go to two very helpful sources. One is a ticket agency. They charge a small fee for each ticket they secure, but they are likely to have the right contacts to get the best available seats or seats for a sold-out performance. Ticket agencies are often located in first-class hotels; if your guest is staying at a hotel which has a ticket agency, use that one. The other source is the concierge at your visitor's hotel, if the hotel has one. A concierge is a very knowledgeable arranger. All world-class European hotels have a concierge; many hotels that cater to business people in America are adding concierges to their staffs. The job of the concierge is to ease the guest's way in the city.

Before making seat reservations for concerts or the theater, you might want to ask your visitors where in the house they like to sit. Some prefer the balcony, some the orchestra. Without promising a particular location, explain that you will try to arrange for tickets as close to their preference as possible. Because of the lateness of these arrangements at times, you may wish to have the ticket agency deliver the tickets to your guest's hotel rather than to the office.

With a party of several people, the earlier the reservations are made, the more likely you will be able to secure a block of seats. In general, a block of seats three or four wide but two or three rows deep is preferable to a long line across a single row. It keeps your party together as a unit.

Tickets should be given to each member of the party ahead of time, at the restaurant if they are eating together, or in their hotel message boxes. If you wait until arrival at the theater or arena to distribute tickets, someone is sure to be missing or late. Someone will have to wait outside for that person.

Your boss may have a business trip to a city with an activity he would like to attend—from opera to boxing—and ask you to make some arrangements. You can call the front desk of his hotel there and ask whether they have a concierge. If so, ask the concierge to make the arrangements for your boss. If they have no concierge, ask for the name and telephone number of the ticket agent with whom they do the most business. Call the agent for information and reservations.

It is not unusual for excellent seats to be available at the last minute; it is not wise, however, to count on them turning up.

CHAPTER SEVEN

Express Services

Most of your contact with out-of-town people will be by regular mail or by telephone. Either the matter is so urgent that a telephone call is required, or there is no rush, in which case an extra day or two in mail delivery makes no significant difference.

Since a business letter costs over eight dollars, it is sometimes less expensive and much easier to make a two- or three-minute telephone call to clear up a matter. However, your boss will usually want a letter written if the matter requires a record, or may even dictate a confirmation letter to follow up the telephone conversation.

Sometimes you will have to send a letter or package that absolutely must reach the recipient that very day or early the next day. You now need to use the right express service.

Messenger

Messengers deliver letters and parcels in a citywide area. Your firm may be large enough to employ someone who works as a messenger when needed. It is more usual, however, to use a messenger service. Your company may have an account with one of the messenger services in town. You either call the service directly with your request, or ask whoever coordinates messenger services in your company to provide the service you need.

If the package has to arrive by a specific time—rather than just in the "late morning" or "early afternoon"—you need to make that clear when you place your order. Since messengers usually try to batch deliveries and pickups by areas of the city—delivering

---

Tip

    Sometimes you will have to send a letter or package that absolutely has to reach the recipient that very day or early the next day. You now need to use the right express service.

---

and picking up at several locations in the same vicinity—any special-priority package needs to be specifically identified.

Couriers

In larger cities, courier services can arrange for hand delivery of packages to other cities or to overseas sites. Your company will be required to pay the airfare—or part of the airfare, if the courier is delivering on behalf of several companies—and the courier service fee.

Courier services are normally used only when the package is of exceptional value or importance. Find a courier service in the yellow pages of the telephone directory or by referral through a district traffic office of a major airline.

Express Mail

The U.S. Postal Service offers an overnight Express Mail service. Rates are the same to any location in the country and are based on the weight of the package. Two rate schedules are in effect: one for delivery to the recipient's location, a lower one for delivery to a post office location. If your recipient uses a post office box for mail delivery, the lower rate is just as quick, since the post office normally does not deliver Express Mail to the business or home address of post office box holders. Before sending Express Mail, check with the post office about a number of variables:

1. Does the Postal Service offer Express Mail service to the zip-code location to which you have addressed the package?

2. What is the cutoff time for you to deliver the package to your post office for overnight delivery to be guaranteed?

3. If you want Saturday or Sunday delivery, is it available at your recipient's location?

One major disadvantage of Express Mail is that you have to deliver the package to the post office in order to get it into the system. Although the Postal Service delivers Express Mail, it does not pick Express Mail up from your office unless you hold a post-office box. However, your office mail room might handle this.

United Parcel Service

The largest national parcel-delivery service is United Parcel Service. UPS makes arrangements for both pickup and delivery. Unless your company has a regular account with UPS and is on a daily pickup schedule, a fee is charged for pickups each week they are made. This fee is added to the delivery charges for the first pickup of each week in which pickups are requested. Arrangements for pickup can be made by using a toll-free UPS telephone number. Pickup normally occurs the day following the call requesting it. Find out from your UPS operations center the latest time you can call in for next-day pickup.

UPS has entered the guaranteed overnight air-express delivery service. Its rates (at time of writing) are excellent for larger, heavier packages and less competitive for letter-type deliveries. UPS does not serve as many locations as some other overnight air-express services. Since this is a highly competitive service, keep up-to-date on rates and locations served regularly.

Overnight Air-Express Service

Several major overnight air-express services are available. Two of the largest and best-known are Federal Express and Emery & Purolator Courier. Express services arrange for both pickup and delivery, using toll-free telephone numbers for pickup arrangements or service inquiries.

Normally you can call in as late as 4 P.M. for same-day pickup and next-day delivery. The time may vary forward or backward a bit, depending on your location. These companies have radios in their delivery vans and require their drivers to call in regularly, so last-minute pickups are part of their service.

Express companies operate their own fleets of airplanes, which converge at a single location during the night, carrying all the packages collected by the vans during the day. Overnight the packages are sorted and sent back by plane to regional distribu-

tion centers, from which they are transported by van to the delivery addresses. Thus, a package sent from Los Angeles to San Francisco is likely to go overnight from L.A. to Memphis. There it is put on the San Francisco plane and delivered by van midmorning the next day.

Most of these companies provide their own mailers and boxes to make it easier for you to package an express delivery for them. You'll have to fill out their airbill (a form requesting your name and address, account number to be charged, your recipient's name and address, and delivery instructions) for each item you send. When you establish an account with an air-express company, they will give you a supply of airbills with your account number, company name, and address preprinted on the forms. You need fill in only the sections relating to the recipient and shipping instructions. A copy of the final airbill, with charges for the delivery, is enclosed in your statement from the express company so you can pass on express charges to a customer, as appropriate.

Each express service publishes a regular listing of zip-code areas served and notes any unusual extra services available or limited services, where appropriate. When you call the toll-free number for a pickup, you are asked for your account number. The operator enters this into a computer, which instantly shows your name, address, and particulars of locations (second floor, for instance, and time of closing). The operator will confirm with you that these particulars are still in effect. Then the operator will give you a confirmation number, such as "NZW 95." This means that you are customer number 95 for the NZW route for the day. If you have a problem with pickup arrangements, use this confirmation number when you call the company's toll-free number to find out why the pickup has not been made by the expected time.

When the driver picks up the package, you will be given a copy of the airbill. Use the airbill number to trace the whereabouts of any package that did not arrive when you expected it. Perhaps as many as five percent of all packages may be lost or delayed, often due to adverse weather conditions. The airbill numbers are recorded at each stage of delivery: from the van to the distribution center, from distribution center to central-sorting center, from central-sorting center to the addressee's distribution center, from that distribution center to the van, and from the van to your company. Within minutes of your call to the toll-free number, you can know who last handled the package and whether it is on the van that serves your recipient. Since these companies are in fierce competition with one another, the percentage of packages misrouted or delivered later than midday is continually being reduced.

These services offer guaranteed overnight or priority delivery for a premium rate. They also offer standard air-delivery rates, which guarantee two-day delivery and usually provide overnight delivery. These rates are about half of the guaranteed overnight delivery rates. If a couple of days is good enough, use the standard rate.

International

Both the U.S. Postal Service and the air-express services offer deliveries to overseas addresses. Depending on the nature of the package, expect some delays for customs clearance. And remember that some countries are more efficient in releasing packages from customs than others.

Always let your recipient know that such a package has been sent, with airbill or Express Mail number, so arrangements can be made at the receiving end to speed up release from the authorities.

Airlines

Airlines offer package and letter (parcel) service. This often means you have to make arrangements for the package to be delivered to the airline counter or cargo office at the airport, and your recipient has to make arrangements to have it picked up at the airport of destination.

This option does mean, however, that a particularly crucial package can be delivered by you at the end of a business day to the airline at the airport, flown to the city of destination, and picked up there on arrival. The cost is usually less than an overnight air-express service since you and your recipient are serving as your own delivery and pickup services.

Tip
Each express service publishes a regular listing of zip-code areas served and notes any extra services available or limited services, where appropriate.

Airlines serving overseas locations also offer package and parcel service, but here arrangements may have to be made for customs clearance through a customs brokerage company. An airline normally uses a company of its own choosing when the sender has not specifically named one. Unless your recipient knows how to utilize such a company—which also charges standard fees for paperwork, high for a small package of relatively little value—it is more convenient for your recipient if you use International Express Mail or one of the air-express services.

Telegrams and Electronic Mail

Years ago, Western Union (WU) dominated the overnight (or faster) express message market. WU offered almost instant telegraphic service from office to office, slightly longer service when using a messenger (including the famous "singing telegram"), and overnight service in what was called a "night letter."

With deregulation of the communications utilities and the advent of new technologies, the Western Union telegram is no longer the only option available for short messages or money orders. Western Union's services are more likely to be found in the form of franchised agencies that handle telegrams and money orders as a part-time extra business than in the form of WU offices in every town and neighborhood. And deliveries are more likely to be by telephone, with a mailed confirmation copy of the message, than by uniformed messenger. But call your nearest WU office to find out the nature of the services available for rapid message transmittal. Radio Corporation of America (RCA) handles a wide range

of overseas message traffic. If your community has an RCA office, find out the nature of their services.

The Postal Service provides overnight electronic mail. Services vary, depending on the location of both the sending and receiving locations. Since these services are growing rapidly, find out the current state of services from your local post office. Electronic mail is a message sent from one computer to another—often by satellite, or else by telephone or radio transmission—printed out by the receiving computer on a message form and delivered by the Postal Service. Since many advertisers use electronic mail, an urgent message delivered by electronic mail sometimes does not convey the same sense of urgency that a Western Union night letter once did.

When originating telegrams, overseas cables, or Postal Service electronic mail, you have to get the message to the transmitting company. Often this can be done over the telephone, with the charge for the service eventually showing up on your telephone bill. Sometimes you can have an account with the transmitting company and receive a monthly statement for messages sent during the previous month. Or you may have to take the message physically to the transmitting company's office and pay for the cost of its transmittal then and there.

A growing alternative for larger companies for interoffice mail handling is internal electronic mail. Computers—mainframe, minicomputers, microcomputers, word processors, personal computers, and the like—are connected to each other by "communications." They can send messages back and forth either in a batch during day or night or at the actual time of the communication, permitting people at either end to type out short messages to each other. A normal way for electronic mail to be sent in a computer-integrated company (one office in San Francisco is "integrated" with the New York office by a communications hookup between computers) is for messages to be sent over a telephone line from computer to computer during the night. First thing in the morning, you or your boss can call up on your screen any messages that were sent in overnight. You can get a hard-copy printout of these messages if you wish, and file and send any replies for communication back to the originating office. If your office has—or enters—this integrated electronic office system, you will receive instructions on how to operate it for your own firm's electronic mail.

The message is no different from what it would normally be when using paper. You compose it or read it on a screen; you "open" it by pressing a couple of keys. It is just a little harder to say, "It must have been lost in the mail."

CHAPTER EIGHT

International Correspondence

Your boss may have regular correspondence with overseas companies or colleagues. In general, international correspondence calls for the same basic rules as all business correspondence: one topic per letter with clear, direct, concrete language. However, keep a number of special points in mind when handling incoming or outgoing overseas correspondence. Much depends on how well the overseas correspondent knows English, on which kind of English he knows, whether English is his second language, and what his native language is. These factors determine how well he uses and understands English, and whether his English has any unusual quirks you need to remember.

Characteristics of Language Use

Sending and Receiving

Every user of a language is both a sender and receiver. You probably understand many more words that you hear or read than you normally use in your own speech or writing. You recognize them or guess their general meaning, even though you may not use them as working words in your everyday vocabulary. This is also true for grammatical forms. You can sense when grammar is correct or when it is less formal, even though you may have forgotten all the special names for verb forms or rules for dealing with gerunds. Usually we are more at home with spoken than with written language.

Levels of Formality

We use language at different levels of formality. An executive addressing the annual meeting of a company's stockholders uses a different level of vocabulary and grammar than he does when telling a joke at a backyard barbecue. On a job interview, he uses more formal language than he does when he describes the interview to a close friend.

Levels of Education

"Educated language" is used in formal and informal situations by someone with many years of formal education. A college professor lecturing to a scholarly organization uses educated, formal language; he tells friends about his vacation in educated, informal language. In his lecture, he uses technical or literary words in which he is not likely to describe his vacation. High-level educated language—doctors talking about medicine, lawyers discussing a legal case, computer scientists comparing high-technology developments—consists of technical words that provide accuracy and serve as abbreviations in rapid communication between specialists. These words are usually unintelligible to those outside the specialty.

"Uneducated language" is used by people with limited formal education. They may speak street language in a big city, or mountain language in a rural community. People who use uneducated language are not ignorant—and may, in fact, be brilliant—but their language is a result not of formal education, but of their living environment.

This language, too, has special words that make speech colorful, and unintelligible to outsiders.

Level for Business Correspondence

Write most of your business correspondence in the common areas of English: those shared by both educated and uneducated users. This guarantees the greatest degree of communication. Many people fail to understand very educated, formal writing; readers may reject slangy, informal correspondence as inappropriate, or feel it is unimportant.

If your letter is about a technical subject, you will probably use special words "insiders" know, which are generally not in the common area of the language. In this kind of letter, some sections will be written in the technical business-correspondence level of language.

Users of English as a Second Language

If your overseas correspondent learned English as a second language, in school, his English may be very stiff. He will tend to apply strict dictionary meanings to words, often using the primary dictionary definition.

He will use grammar in a precise, but not always accurate or idiomatic way. You may sometimes have the feeling a schoolchild is writing. Don't be misled by this; the correspondent may be brilliant in his field and gifted in his own language but have limited knowledge of English vocabulary and grammar. He needs to be understood at the level of his professional and business competence, not underestimated because of his limited English fluency. His "window" on

> **Tip**
>
>   We use language at different levels of formality. An executive addressing the annual meeting of a company's stockholders uses a different level of vocabulary and grammar than he does when telling a joke at a backyard barbecue. On a job interview, his language is more formal than it is when he describes the interview to a close friend.

the range of English is smaller than that of a native English user. It is the kind of English taught in high school and university. He also knows the specialized English used in his professional and business work. Since English is widely used internationally for science and business, his proficiency in professional language is probably greater than his skill in general usage. Of course, the more exposure he has to English, the larger his "window" will become.

From Romance-Language Areas

If your correspondent is from an area speaking a Romance language (Spanish, French, Italian, Portuguese—languages that grew out of Latin), stay alert to possible misunderstandings, arising because many English words are based on Latin roots. Even though they share the same Latin origin, words developed differently in English than they did in Spanish or French, for instance.

Your Spanish correspondent writing in English may mention the "rentability" of a new product. To a native English speaker, that suggests leasing the product or renting it out. However, your correspondent bases his understanding of the word "rentability" on the root *rendita*, meaning "income in general" or "profit," so what he has in mind when he says "rentability" is expressed in English by "profitability." (Incidentally, the English word "rent" came from an Old French word *rente*, which meant "income from property"—a meaning that has remained in English; in French, the word *rente* has expanded to include the concepts of "income," "dividends," and "interest," as well as "profit.")

Sometimes words have such different ranges of meaning that they can be misleading. In Spanish, the word *profesor* refers to any teacher—from kindergarten teacher up to elite university posts. In English, the word "professor" is only for university or college teachers, except when used colloquially to refer to a person of some unusual skill. You may get quite the wrong meaning from your correspondent's letter if you automatically assume he uses the word in the English sense.

A frequent example is the word "rationalize." In American English this means to "explain away" or "justify to oneself." But a Spanish-language user (or even a British-English user) bases his use of the word on the root meaning "rational," in the sense of to "think about," so he uses the word to mean "make organized and logical sense of something and put matters into a logical and coherent framework." When he wants to "rationalize" an organization, he wants to restructure it according to a logical analysis. You can readily see how an American and his overseas correspondent can get quite confused by the different meanings they find in the same word.

Technical Words

Highly technical words are usually clear to both parties, since they share a common international scientific and professional vocabulary. Accountants mean the same thing by "credit" or "debit"; all physiologists understand "enzymes" or "hormones" identically. Your awareness of cross-cultural communication will help you grasp the content of overseas correspondence more accurately. It can let you alert your boss to a possible problem when you see confusion brewing.

If you correspond regularly with people from a certain language area—even though the correspondence takes place in English—keep a bilingual dictionary at hand. When you see an expression that looks normal but does not really make sense, look up key words in the dictionary. You'll usually find one of the possible definitions does make sense, even though your first interpretation was unclear. When sending correspondence to foreigners for whom English is a second language, use the same "window" of moderately formal, dictionary-definition English. Use the first and obvious definition of the word rather than literary or figurative meanings. Straightforward clarity is better than subtle use of the language, which will only confuse your reader.

Above all, avoid everyday American slang or colloquial language. A Pakistani correspondent, for instance, knows the meaning of "hot" and of "dog." But unless he lived in America, he probably doesn't know what a "hot dog" is. He almost surely doesn't know the meaning of "Hot dog!" (an expression of great joy or enthusiasm), nor does he describe a person with a showy style of skateboarding or skiing as "a hot dog."

British English

If your correspondent is a native British-English user—whether from England, Nigeria, India, Singapore, or New Zealand—cross-cultural communication is easier, but still cannot be taken for granted. Formal dictionary definitions of everyday words show some confusing differences. British "corn" is American "wheat"; American "corn" is British "maize." British "tin" is American "can" (of vegetables); American "thread" is British "cotton" (for sewing). British "bonnet" is American "hood" (of automobile [British "motor car"]); American "trunk" is British "boot" (in the same automobile); but American "trunk" is also British "portmanteau" (a large, hinged container for packing clothes when traveling).

With slang or informal idioms, the different meanings of American and British En-

---

Tip

If your overseas correspondent learned English as a second language, in school, his English may be very stiff. He will use grammar in a precise, but not always accurate or idiomatic way. You may sometimes have the feeling a schoolchild is writing. Don't be misled by this; the correspondent may be brilliant in his field and gifted in his own language but have limited knowledge of English vocabulary and grammar. He needs to be understood at the level of his professional and business competence, not underestimated because of his limited English fluency.

glish increase considerably. This explains why Americans seldom laugh at British jokes (and the other way around); jokes are usually a play on words at the informal level. When the meaning of the words has to be explained, the cause of the humorous reaction is lost. A joke that has to be explained is no longer funny. George Bernard Shaw once quipped that Americans and the English were separated by the same language. This witticism contains enough truth to warn that business correspondence between American and British English users offers the greatest degree of mutual comprehension when conducted in a kind of "mid-Atlantic" English: standard, direct, unidiomatic language without regional color or the latest word fads.

A Sample Letter

Let's consider an annotated sample of a business letter to an overseas correspondent:

February 15, 1999

Sr. Petro Carcamo-Gonzales
ABC International, S.A.
Apto. 456
123 Avenida del Cinco de Mayo
San Jose, Costa Rica

Dear Sr. Carcamo:

I received your letter of January 3, 1999. In your letter you ask about purchasing software for use in your accounting department.

Our company has an excellent software program for accounting, inventory control, and payroll. Although we developed this software for use on the Zenox business microcomputer, we also have versions for use on other popular microcomputers. In your letter, you did not tell us which microcomputer you use. Please tell me the name of the manufacturer, the model number, and the memory capacity (number of bytes) of your microcomputer, and I will send you complete information about the proper software program for your needs.

I look forward to hearing from you soon.

With every good wish, I remain

Yours sincerely,

John P. Wizard
International Services

> **Tip**
> Overseas correspondents tend to be more flowery than American business-letter writers. Therefore the extra expression of good wishes and personal reference is appropriate.

Note the following characteristics:

- **Date:** Most overseas correspondents use a day/month/year sequence when using only figures. Thus, *12/2/99* is *February 12, 1999*, not *December 2, 1999*, for most people in foreign countries. Avoid possible confusion by spelling out the month.

- **Complimentary title:** Although you can use "Mr." in addressing overseas correspondents, it is more courteous to use the appropriate title in their own language. In this case, *Sr.* stands for *Señor*. You could use *Herr* (German), *M.* (French for *Monsieur*), and so on.

- **Name:** Use the proper form of the person's name. In a Spanish-language man's name, the man's mother's family name is part of his formal name. His father's family name is first, with his mother's family name joined to it by a hyphen. However, when he is addressed directly, only the father's family name is used. Legally and formally he is *Carcamo-Gonzales* (father's family name–mother's family name), but when spoken to directly he is *Señor Carcamo*. A married woman's formal and legal name is made by joining her father's family name and her husband's family name with *y* ("and"), but she is addressed by her husband's name. Thus, *Sra. Teresa Lopez y Carcamo* would be addressed directly as *Sra. Carcamo*.

Other languages have other conventions.

By using them correctly, you show that you care about the person and the traditions of his culture. He may note that you have been polite and correct, if you use his name properly, but he will be sure to notice when you use it improperly. At best, he will laugh at your ignorance; at worst, he may take offense at your carelessness.

- **Box number:** In some languages the word for "Post Office Box" may remind you of some other meaning in English. In Spanish the word is *Apartado* or *Apto*. It is not an "apartment." Because post office personnel in the correspondent's country may not readily understand English, use an address form taken from your correspondent's letterhead to make sure your letter arrives without unnecessary delay.

- **Body of the letter:** Express yourself in clear, direct form. Avoid passive, perfect, and pluperfect tenses as much as possible. Use the present tense, simple past, and simple future tense, but avoid conditional future-tense forms whenever possible. Think of your correspondent as an intelligent person with limited skill in English. Brand names and technical language, however, do not pose any great problem.

- **Closing:** Overseas correspondents tend to be more flowery than American business-letter writers. Therefore the extra expression of good wishes and personal reference is appropriate.

PART THREE

INSIDE THE COMPANY

Another entire set of your secretarial relationships is with people and tasks within the company. Primary, of course, is your relationship with your boss and the work you do to make his job easier and more effective. One of your most significant contributions can be as a buffer, absorbing the little tasks and interruptions that can keep him from performing at his best. You will also relate to other people in the company on behalf of your boss. How you do it can help or hinder your boss's future in the company. Much of your time will be spent in performing standard secretarial tasks. Part III focuses on these relationships and tasks within the company.

CHAPTER NINE

Dictation

Shorthand is a status skill. It gives a secretary prestige, since most clerk-typists do not know how to use shorthand. And it provides status for the boss, since she can occasionally dictate to and interact with another person. It makes her feel good. It may even be useful when short memos or instructions are conveyed. However, in today's electronic office, person-to-person dictating is becoming rare. The dictator may use an office dictating machine that rests on her desk or bookcase, or a portable dictating machine she takes on trips or to her home for overnight or weekend dictating. She may use a centralized telephone system, either from her office phone or from any phone anywhere.

Pool Dictation

The person who transcribes electronic dictation may be the boss's secretary. In larger offices, it may be a pool typist or an operator in the word-processing department. If the transcribing is done by someone other than you, you will have to check the work to make sure it is done properly before you turn it over to your boss to sign.

Beginning Worries

When you first start working with dictation for a new company or a new boss, your main concern will be handling new words that seem to come at you from all sides. Many of these are words you've never heard before, and you wonder whether you'll be able to meet the constant demand to learn them all.

Be concerned, but don't worry. You will encounter two classes of new words: the technical vocabulary of the company and the business the company is in, and the personal vocabulary of your boss. At first you may feel overwhelmed by the number of new words you face, but within a few weeks you will feel at home with them. Remember that the company's technical vocabulary is limited. The same words keep appearing over and over again as product lines and processes are discussed. As you become familiar with these words in your transcribing, you will soon master most of them. Only now and then will you meet a new group of technical words when another product or process is developed. Furthermore, an individual's working vocabulary is also limited. At first it may seem as though your boss knows an exceptionally wide range of words. But as you handle her dictation over hundreds of letters and memos, you will learn that she tends to use the same formulas over and over again. Once you are familiar with the patterns of her dictation, you will have little trouble with unknown words catching you off guard. Soon you will be so familiar with both the company's and your boss's vocabularies that you will be able to write a letter on a routine subject in your boss's style with very little difficulty. After you have done this a few times, your boss may routinely tell you to write a letter, giving you the gist of what she wants included and letting you put the letter together.

Your Own Word List

As you begin learning the special vocabularies of your company and boss, look up every unfamiliar word in a dictionary to make sure you have the spelling right. You may even want to keep your own speller-divider list in a handy drawer, adding to it as you meet new, repeated words. Having such a list close by will save the time and effort of looking up words each time you encounter them, until you have mastered them. If you use a word processor with a dictionary or spell-check feature to which you can add words, add these words. Then whenever you spell-check a letter with your word processor, the new words will automatically be included in the checking.

First Copy as Final Copy

For regular letters and memos, prepare your first copy as your final copy for your boss's signature. These letters are expensive (considering your boss's time, your time, and machine costs, as well as the cost of postage, paper, and ribbon), so a draft copy for a routine letter is an unnecessary luxury.

First Copy as Draft Copy

For longer, highly complex letters, memos, and reports, a draft copy (double-spaced for editing convenience) is probably best. When she sees the copy in print, your boss can usually spot corrections that she did not sense when she was dictating.

Dictating Reference Needs

Make dictation easier for your boss by attaching all needed resource or reference material to the letter or memo she is answering. This includes the file of any previous correspondence to the person, and any reports or studies referred to by the correspondent in the letter. Give your boss any additional names and addresses referred to in the answer.

Tip

An individual's working vocabulary is limited. At first it may seem as though your boss knows an exceptionally wide range of words. But as you handle her dictation over hundreds of letters and memos, you will learn that she tends to use the same formulas over and over again.

Final Form

Have your boss clearly indicate at the beginning what form any dictation should take: letter, memo, report. She should specify the type of stationery: letterhead (and type of letterhead if she uses more than one), interoffice memo, plain.

She should tell you the number of copies needed. (This is more important to know at the very beginning if carbon paper will be used; it is less important if you will be making photocopies.)

Retention of Original

If you use a word processor, your boss should tell you how long she wants the original retained on a diskette or in the central memory unit. She would normally only want to retain a copy in electronic form if she plans to revise the letter sometime in the near future.

Punctuation

Work out a system with your boss about punctuation. She can dictate each punctuation mark. If she does dictate punctuation marks, you have to be careful not to type out the name of the punctuation as you move along. It can be aggravating to type out the word "period" when the rest of your copy is completely clean. It is probably best for her to indicate any special punctuation she wants, ends of sentences, and ends of paragraphs. Other than that she may want you to punctuate the rest of the letter as needed. Use one of the usage manuals listed in the appendix for simple rules on present-day punctuation. Generally speaking, fewer commas are used now than twenty-five years ago. If your boss is older, she may feel more comfortable with more commas. Either way is correct; it's a matter of personal preference and overall style. You will quickly gain a good sense of how your boss likes her dictation punctuated.

Enclosures

Have your boss specify, as part of her dictation, any enclosures to be sent with the letter. Your problem is to make sure the enclosures actually go out with the letter. It is easy to have the letter signed along with several others, slip it in an envelope, and mail it without the enclosures. The best way to insure enclosures are not forgotten is to gather them and give them to your boss as a complete package with the correspondence to be signed and the envelope. Your boss will leaf through them, too, which serves as a double check that all enclosures have been gathered. If the complete package is too bulky, then add a different-colored sheet of paper (yellow, for instance) that lists each enclosure you have collected. The different color reminds you to put the correspondence and the enclosures together when the signed correspondence is sent out for you to mail.

Distribution of Copies

Have your boss specify copy distribution at the time of dictation. For outside distribution, she may have to include the name and address. Company addressees will receive copies by interoffice mail. If your boss sends someone copies of several different letters, it is wise to keep an envelope open for that person throughout the day. Keep adding the copies as they become available, and send the envelope at the close of the day. This is especially important with copies for outside parties because you will want to keep mail costs as low as possible.

Spare Batteries

If your boss uses a portable dictating unit operated by batteries, keep an extra supply of batteries on hand so you can replace them when they run low. She may not know that the batteries are giving out. You will be aware first because the unit will run slowly, sometimes unevenly, and her voice will sound lower and increasingly distorted.

Soundalike Words

Many words in English sound alike but are spelled differently. These soundalikes have very different meanings. If she is alert to the problem they might cause, your boss will spell out the one she wants. But more often than not, she does not think of the other word while she's dictating. You can generally figure out which one is right by the context in which it appears. Occasionally you may have to ask her which one she wants. Here are some soundalikes that can easily appear in business correspondence:

accede / exceed
accept / except
addition / edition
access / excess
affect / effect
assistants / assistance
brake / break
coarse / course
cite / sight / site
complement / compliment
correspondents / correspondence
council / counsel / consul
incidents / incidence
its / it's
legislator / legislature
loose / lose
passed / past
personal / personnel
principle / principal
respectfully / respectively
right / write
stationary / stationery
their / there / they're
whose / who's
your / you're

You will develop your own list of soundalikes that occur in your boss's dictation and in the company's vocabulary. Keep in mind that it's *(its? it's?)* the little ones which cause the most trouble in you're *(your* is the correct choice here) typing—see what I mean?

Correction Marks

Work out a standard form for indicating corrections with your boss, so you both know what she wants done when she returns a letter for revision. Both of you do not have to learn all the standard proof-reader's marks, but some of their symbols are helpful. (The full set of marks can be found in most college and office dictionaries). The usual kinds of corrections in business correspondence can be easily noted with these standard marks:

to entirely change your	Transpose words or letters
me send your order	Insert word(s)
	Move to left
	Move to right
	Center on page
9th or NJ	Spell out (ninth or New Jersey)
the President of IBM	Put in lower case (small letters)—president
the president will then	Put in upper case (caps)—President
However the company will	Insert comma (or semicolon)
The answer is yes	Insert period (or colon)
book keeper	Close up
# The answer is yes	Add space
¶	Start new paragraph here
call you tomorrow. Then we can decide	Run in; no paragraph
to entirely change	Delete; remove word(s) or letters

CHAPTER TEN

Your Boss's Calendar

Your boss has several important assets: professional knowledge, time, and colleagues in the company and in his field. Your work in correspondence and file maintenance will help him bring professional knowledge to bear on his job; your reception and telephone work will help advance his relationships with his company and colleagues. Your monitoring of his calendar can help him use his time in the best possible way.

The Importance of Time

The importance of an executive's time cannot be stressed enough. Every activity he engages in is at the cost of something else he could have been doing. If your careful monitoring of his calendar can enable him to do fifteen things during the day instead of twelve (or to do those twelve things better because he was less hassled since more time was available to consider them), you have helped both him and the company significantly.

Who Keeps the Master Calendar

The first matter you and your boss need to agree on is who keeps the master calendar. Normally you will have a daily calendar on your desk; he will carry a pocket calendar with him. (He may have a large executive desk calendar that shows a week on a two-page spread, in addition to the pocket calendar.) One of these should be designated as the master calendar. Entries into the other calendars are tentative until posted on the master calendar, with any conflicts resolved. He may wish to keep the master calendar, asking you to present requests that come in by telephone or mail for him to decide upon and enter on his calendar. Or he may ask you to keep it up-to-date, reserving the right to change it from time to time as he sees fit, and asking you to rearrange appointments that have to be changed. He will certainly want to retain the right to make any appointment he wishes or to change them as he deems best. However, he may also give you the responsibility of making appointments for him. If he does, it is even more important to update all calendars regularly. This avoids the embarrassment of double-booking and enables him to cancel any appointment you have made for him that he does not want to keep at that time.

The Day in Fifteen-Minute Segments

It is useful to think of your boss's day in fifteen-minute segments (naturally, such a time division is only a guide; very seldom will your boss actually operate on such a tight, regimented schedule). Most people in the company can transact their business in one or two such fifteen-minute segments, usually one. No leisurely get-acquainted period is needed, as it is with a new outside visitor. Nor does a company visitor have to brief your boss in detail about the problem; it is often well-known to both and this visit is just a continuing consultation about an ongoing matter.

In-Company Visitors

You can ask the person in the company who wants to see your boss how long he expects to take. By asking this, you alert him to the need to keep the visit brief and remind him that your boss has other commitments making demands upon his time. (Of course, you ask this only of people equal to or lower than your boss in company rank; your boss's boss has the privilege of immediate and untimed access.) Your regular in-company visitor may say, "I just want to see him for two minutes." Generally, you can count on five, and often it will run on to fifteen. If your boss is really pressed for time, stress that to the visitor. Your boss may be too polite to end the visit as soon as he should to keep the rest of the day in control, especially if the visitor is in the midst of telling the latest joke making the office rounds after having finished his business.

Outside Visitors

A visitor from the outside may require two to four fifteen-minute segments. Unless the visit is connected to a lunch date,

---

Tip
Your boss has several important assets: professional knowledge, colleagues in the company and in his field, and time.

> **Tip**
>
> The importance of an executive's time cannot be stressed enough. Every activity is engaged in at the cost of something else that could have been done.

---

most business can be conducted in an hour. If a lunch arrangement is involved, schedule the business visit for the hour before lunch whenever possible. Any remaining matters are usually discussed during lunch, without the visitor returning to the office after the meal. If, however, that hour is already scheduled, your boss can meet the person at the restaurant or in your reception room or in his office a few minutes before leaving for lunch. Business will usually be the main agenda at lunch, and any unfinished matters can be dealt with back at the office after lunch. Because a luncheon meeting may tend to last longer than when the same amount of business is conducted in an office, keep a little leeway in the calendar for the time after lunch. You should remind your boss, however, if he has an appointment soon after the normal lunch hour. That will give him a reason for closing the lunchtime discussion in time to make his next appointment.

Tentative Appointments

People often say they will "pencil" in an appointment, meaning that they are setting it tentatively, to be confirmed at a later time. The idea is that a penciled entry on a calendar can be readily erased in case of a conflict. This may be a useful practice for you to adopt. Enter in pencil tentative dates or appointments to be cleared with your boss or others; write firm appointments in ink. By adopting this method, you can tell at a glance which appointments still await confirmation or clearance.

When Your Boss Is Running Late

When you see that your boss is running late—either with in-house appointments or with meetings or a lunch date outside the office—and that scheduled appointments are going to be jammed or will have to be postponed, find out from your boss, if possible, which ones to put off until later. Call those people and give them a new time, or indicate that your boss sends his apologies for canceling the appointment now and will get back to them later about setting up a new one. If your boss is not available at the time you see schedule trouble brewing, call the people immediately affected and tell them that your boss is running late and you will get back to them after you have the opportunity of seeing your boss. You might need to reschedule the appointment. This courtesy will be much appreciated by your boss and by the person whose appointment is affected. Your boss won't have to apologize for keeping the person waiting or for causing him to make a fruitless trip. The prospective visitor will be flattered that your boss thought enough of him to have you call.

> **Tip**
>
> Who your boss sees and where they go for lunch is his business. You should not volunteer this information if someone calls and wants to know where he is. If the lunch date goes on until 3:30 P.M., never tell the caller that your boss isn't back from lunch yet.

Who Should Know About Your Boss's Schedule

Who your boss sees and where they go for lunch is his business. You should not volunteer this information if someone calls and wants to know where he is. If the lunch date goes on until 3:30 P.M., don't tell the caller that your boss isn't back from lunch yet. Just say that he isn't available at present and ask for information so your boss can call back later. Most callers will wait until well into the early afternoon before calling. They can be irritated if told your boss is still out to lunch, and don't really want to hear he only just left for lunch ten minutes ago. Your office schedule is of little interest to them; they just want to talk to your boss.

Appointment Courtesies

An out-of-town visitor usually tries to have four or five business appointments during each day he is in town in order to make the trip as worthwhile as possible. This is especially true if he is in town only for the day and must include airline schedules and traffic congestion to the airport in his planning. Anything you and your boss can do to accommodate his timing request will be much appreciated by the visitor. He will understand that meetings and earlier commitments cannot be adjusted, but he will also be grateful for your meeting his requests as closely as possible. And your boss may hope for the same kind of accommodation when he sets up an itinerary for his out-of-town business trips.

As a courtesy for out-of-town visitors, keep a map of your city and general area in your desk. From time to time a visitor will have to go to another office he has never visited before and doesn't know how to reach from your office. You may not know how yourself, but being able to look at local maps for a few minutes might save your visitor valuable time and much anguish. If he is running a little late, offer him the use of a telephone to call his next appointment. This will save him the time and anxiety of looking for a public telephone somewhere in your building or in some public place outside.

Appointments with Juniors

When your boss asks you to make an appointment with someone who works for him, it is courteous to let the person know the general subject your boss wants to discuss. This allows the person to prepare himself, making the meeting more productive for both people. Otherwise, the person may wonder whether he is being called on the carpet or even faces dismissal. Imagination can create all sorts of unpleasant scenarios. And unless your boss has such an unpleasant task to perform, a summons to his office need not arouse free-floating anxiety. The person may have enough to do to get ready to see your boss without carrying the weight of the unknown.

Appointments with Peers and Seniors

Normally your boss will make his own appointments with his boss and peers. Occasionally he may ask you to call the other person's secretary to see if that person might be free for lunch or at a particular hour. Then your boss will probably use that information when making the appointment.

Office Appearance

The general appearance of your office and your boss's office is an advertisement about how you run your business. A sloppy office suggests to the visitor that he will suffer from sloppy treatment in the long run. A cold, austere atmosphere implies the visitor will be treated with little human warmth or understanding. A neat, but obviously active workplace with touches of personal interest tells a visitor he will be treated personally and efficiently by a busy but in-control company. The amount of personal decorating you can introduce into your own work space is dictated by company policy and the office environment. In a large office with standardized modules and work spaces carefully coordinated by an office designer, you'll have little opportunity for much personalization of your own space. A photograph or two, a hanging calendar or poster, some flowers or personal accessories on your desk are the most that will normally be allowed, or acceptable, in a standardized, designed office. In a smaller, older office, you can bring a few more personal effects to create your own space. However, your office should not become your "home away from home." Leave your home at home, and make your office a pleasant, cheerful working place.

If you are located outside your boss's office, rather than in your own office, you will have fewer choices. They should be discussed with her, since they serve as an entry to her own office. Here I am talking more about a dramatic, colorful poster on the wall than about a small family picture on your desk or the choice of desk accessories. Since you have to spend eight hours of each working day in this office, you want it to look as pleasing and relaxing as possible. You also have to consider the fact that it is a place where others spend eight hours of their working days. The degree to which you can personalize your environment increases as you move from a pool situation, to an office-related wall, to your own office.

Included in your personal effects is your own professional bookshelf. This should include books about secretarial usage and practice, wordbooks and dictionaries, stylebooks, and professional or trade books about your company's business. Some of these books will be provided by the company; others are your own. Readily available, they make a pleasing appearance against a stark wall. As they become well used, they give an impression of professionalism to passing visitors.

As you work, you tend to spread papers and files around you. Each time you finish a particular job, put the papers and files away before starting on the next job. This way the clutter never gets out of control. Before lunch and at the end of each day, do a general tidying up. This is the time to pick up stray paper clips, put the adhesive tape back where you usually keep it, return extra pencils to the drawer or pencil holder, cover your typewriter or dust your word processor, and put all your diskettes in their proper place.

You can keep your own work space neat and organized. You will have less control over the appearance of your boss's office. Much depends on whether she is a "clean desk" or "cluttered desk" type. Your job will be greatly simplified if she leans toward the clean-desk habit. She will then regularly give you files of papers to sort through and handle. If, however, she tends to be more cluttered, you will have to work out with her a mutually agreeable pattern for handling her papers. Does she, for example, want you to go through the papers on her desk every day to remove those no longer needed and put in order those she is working on? You may even have to remind her, now and then, about the relative urgency of a paper you discovered lying at the bottom of a pile that should have been acted on earlier. The clutter type of boss tends, now and then, to lose track of a piece of paper. Part of your job is to know what on her desk is still pending so when questions come up about it, you can find it and bring it to your boss's attention. With the clutter type, keep moving as many papers as you can from her desk into the files. You can always get them again if they are needed. The clutter type will tend to hold on to papers for longer than she needs them rather than send them out for filing when she should. Your discreet management of her desktop will not only keep her office looking neater, but also provide better long-term management of her paperwork.

Tip

Your office should not become your "home away from home." Leave your home at home, and make your office a pleasant, cheerful working place.

Tip

You can keep your own work space neat and organized. You will have less control over the appearance of your boss's office.

In keeping both your own and your boss's office generally neat, you should not take on maintenance and cleaning jobs. Let the office cleaners do their work. But when you see a noticeable problem that is not likely to resolve itself, initiate a solution. If, for instance, a visitor spills a cup of coffee over a sofa and onto the rug, bring the matter to the attention of the maintenance department so it can be thoroughly cleaned before the stains set. If a chair leg breaks, that, too, should be called to the attention of the maintenance department for repair or replacement. Make the system work to provide the right level of maintenance. For this reason, it is good to develop a supportive, rather than a critical relationship with the head of the maintenance department. Much more can be accomplished with a show of personal regard than can often be done through formal memos or complaining phone calls.

CHAPTER TWELVE

Dress for Success

Several books are available on dressing for success in the business world. Most are written for people who have had little exposure to the business environment and hope their clothes will make a statement about their professional capability. They are also written for those with little confidence in their own clothes sense who seek guidance from people far more experienced in the business world. However confident you feel in your own clothes decisions and however much you have set your own style, a brief glance through one of these books can be enlightening and helpful. You can make the mistake of dressing below the level of responsibility you have. If you have been promoted from a clerk-typist position, or from a typing or word-processing pool, you have probably dressed to fit in with your peers. Now you've moved up in the company and that style of dress may no longer be advisable in your new position.

Consider, too, the rank your boss holds in the company and dress in a way that he, his visitors, and peers might think appropriate. You may have to switch from faded denims to flannel slacks, from pants to skirts, from casual sportswear to suits and blazers, or from athletic shoes to street shoes. Appropriate dress has no clear, standardized formula. The once critical rules gave way in recent years to a great deal of flexibility. Much also depends on the region of the country in which you work. For instance, I now work and live near the ocean where the "uniform of the day" includes boating shoes.

> **Tip**
>
> It is important not to underdress for your position in the company; it is also important not to overdress.

I wear them to work; my dentist wears them at his office; my lawyer wears them at his; my accountant wears them when he calls on me, as does my banker when I visit him. However, when I visit clients in New York or Boston, I do not wear boating shoes. Nor do people who work in a nonboating region—say, Denver—wear boating shoes as part of their working dress. Dress-for-success suggestions are generally directed to people who want to succeed in the major cities of the country. Adapt their suggestions to the conditions in the region where you work. If it is important not to underdress for your position in the company, it is also vital not to overdress. The degree of formality in dress appropriate for the secretary of the corporate president may be too overpowering if worn by the secretary of a junior officer. Unwritten dress standards are set by the practice of your region, city, and company. Using your own eyes and sense of good judgment, determine what feels right for your present position, while helping you appear to be a reasonable candidate for a higher position. As your work will create a reputation for you in the company, so will your appearance have an impact on executives in the firm. An air of disciplined, personable efficiency as shown by your dress makes an immediate impression that will cause them to look carefully at your work performance. Inappropriate attire will lead them to take your work less seriously than they would if you dressed appropriately.

If you have a limited clothing budget, look for classics—clothes that don't come and go with each passing season. Keep those fashions for your after-work activities. Buy for quality. Consider natural rather than synthetic fibers, as they are more comfortable, easier to keep clean, and readily show their quality. Choose neutral colors: blacks, tans, blues, grays. Add bright colors in your accessories: blouses, shirts, ties, scarves, sweaters, and so on. A classic blazer, slacks/skirt combination can last for several seasons, with continual change achieved by changing accessories. Quality clothes will hold up well for several seasons, in both condition and style. Inexpensive clothes will fall apart quickly, lose their shape, seldom fit right in the first

> **Tip**
>
> Unwritten dress standards are set by the practice in your region, city, and company. Using your own eyes and sense of good judgment, determine what feels right for your present position, while helping you appear to be a reasonable candidate for a higher position.

place, and become dated quickly. In the long run, it is actually cheaper to buy fewer but better clothes for work than to purchase more but less expensive clothes.

It costs surprisingly little more to buy quality clothes. Study the features of good clothing (stitching, lining, styling, material—see a book from the library on clothing characteristics) and then look for such garments in reputable discount stores. Up to 90 percent of clothing in "off-price" stores is not of the quality you would desire, but if you find that 10 percent and recognize it, you can stretch your clothing dollar. One discount house advertises with the slogan, "An educated consumer is our best customer." Educate yourself about quality in clothing, and you will dress better for less. How you dress for the office also affects how you feel about yourself and your work. If you don't take your job seriously and have a low opinion of yourself, your dress will somehow reflect those feelings. If, however, you feel good about yourself and your job is important to you, your dress will also show those sentiments. In fact, interconnection between your emotions and your attire is so strong that you can help enhance good feelings about yourself and your job by dressing as if you already had those feelings. Then, when you glance at yourself in a window, sense someone looking at you with appreciation, or know how right you look, you will usually grow inwardly into your own expectations. Dress is as much for your morale and sense of self-esteem as it is for your job setting.

CHAPTER THIRTEEN

Guarding the Door

As keeper of the gate, you are the one through whom most people in the company make arrangements to see your boss. Constant decisions have to be made about who to let in, or postpone, or help, or discourage. The conflict is between your boss's need to know what the person has to say or the importance of her answer to the person's questions, and the protection of her time and privacy so she can complete important tasks. A visitor may really need your boss's answers, or may come primarily to call attention to himself on the pretext of asking your boss a business question.

Some bosses have an open-door policy, so that anyone who wants to see them can just walk in. This kind of boss probably remembers the frustrations she felt trying to see her boss, and determined that people who worked with her would always have access. Generally, this works well, except an "open-door" boss is always at the mercy of people who want to see her for frivolous as well as serious matters. Time for concentration on working out her own tasks is always interrupted, adversely affecting the quality of her own output.

Some bosses go to the opposite extreme. Their door is always closed; people can see them only by appointment or summons. They control who they see and when, and you are the receptionist. Somewhere in between is the boss who works behind a closed door when she wants to concentrate or to see someone privately, but opens her door as a sign that people are free to drop by

> **Tip**
>
> When turning a visitor away, do not give the impression that his problem is insignificant or that he does not count.

to see her briefly. This kind of boss is more likely to use you as a guardian of the door.

She may want you to interrupt her when the door is closed but someone comes with a genuine emergency. She may want you to put through a telephone call even though she has a visitor if that call is one she has been trying to complete for some time. But she may also want you to turn away anyone who would interrupt her while she is preparing a report, and tell you to assure them that she will get in touch with them later in the afternoon. She may want you to hold all calls while she has a visitor and have you tell the caller that she will telephone the next morning. This kind of boss will learn to let you make the judgment about the urgency of an interruption as you both get to know each other.

A sensitive problem of guarding the door is the matter of perspective. Your boss—and hence, you—have a much wider view of the company and its priorities than does someone who works in a specialized area under your boss. What that person sees as vital is probably important in the performance of his work or in his level of responsibility in the company. But in your boss's perspective, that person's problem is less crucial than some other problem needing immediate attention.

When turning the visitor away, do not give the impression that his problem is insignificant or that he does not count, even though you know your boss faces more urgent matters at the moment. You must reassure the visitor that your boss will soon get back to him. In fact, your boss may later give you the answer to convey to this person; assure him it is straight from your boss so he continues to feel he was heard at the boss's level. Make sure to bring the concerns of every visitor you turned away or postponed to your boss's attention as soon as you can. Many major problems started as minor ones that were ignored until it was too late.

Some bosses like a diary kept of who they see and for how long. For certain professionals, such as lawyers, this information is important for billing purposes. For other executives it is important for record-keeping. This is particularly true for government officials. If these records are needed or wanted by your boss, she may ask you to note in a diary who comes to see her and the times of their arrival and departure. This diary is different from an appointment book. The appointment book does not detail everyone who slips in and out, nor are all appointments kept as scheduled. The appointment book is the plan of the day; the diary is the record of the actual day itself. Such a diary, if routinely maintained, is acceptable as a legal record of fact.

CHAPTER FOURTEEN

Routines and Reminder Systems

A critical factor in business success is getting things done on time. To do so requires planning, scheduling, and schedule monitoring. These are included in the services a secretary can perform, provided your boss wants you to and that you work together on it.

Routines

Some business tasks are routine, consisting of regularly scheduled tasks, which are to be performed at stated times each day, each week, each month, or each quarter. You and your boss should discuss thoroughly which routine tasks he has to perform, and which he wants you to handle. You should list these on the master calendar.

If the task is rather simple, list it only on the day it is to be done. However, for a task requiring considerable preparation, list the preparation day as well as the day of the task on the master calendar. For instance, if your boss has a monthly heads-of-departments meeting to attend, list the day of the meeting on the calendar. But if it takes him two or three days to prepare for the meeting, you should list "prep: Dept. Heads Mtg." sufficiently ahead of the day of the meeting to leave him adequate preparation time. Just which day or days are preparation time depends on the rest of his schedule during that period. The reasons for using the master calendar to record the due dates for routine tasks are:

1. To avoid having to record dates in different locations.

2. To avoid having to look up dates in different locations.

3. To be able to see the week's work schedule at a glance so the proper amount of time can be allocated for each task. This avoids, as much as possible, hassled, half-done work at the last minute to meet a deadline.

4. To show at a glance the impact an unexpected appointment or business trip will have on the timely accomplishments of the routine tasks due to be performed.

Some secretaries enter the routine tasks in a unique color. All routine tasks, for example are listed in green. This enables you and your boss to tell instantly which entries are appointments and which are tasks to be done. The heads-of-departments meeting would be in blue or black ink, since it is an appointment. Preparation for the meeting would be noted in green, since it is a task to be included in the day's activities.

You and your boss have to work out which routine tasks are his alone, which are yours, and which require you to collect information or do certain preliminaries for him before he can complete the task. As time goes on, you will probably be able to complete an increasing number of routine tasks yourself, freeing your boss for other work.

Reminder Suggestions

Many business tasks are not routine in nature, but the deadline for their performance is known some time in advance. For instance, your boss may have told a major customer he will send advance information about a new line of equipment as soon as Engineering makes a report about the performance of the machinery. Engineering is due to report at the July heads-of-department meeting. Remind your boss to send information to the customer within a day or two after the meeting.

Tickler File

The easiest way to keep track of nonroutine tasks is to keep a "tickler" file, named for the idea of tickling your memory. A tickler file has twelve large folders—one for each month of the year—and thirty-one smaller folders—one for each day of the month. The system is very easy to work with:

1. Write the name of a task and the date it is to be done on a piece of paper and place it in the month file. Or photocopy a piece of correspondence in which the task is discussed, write the date on which it is to be accomplished in large letters, and place the copy in the month file. Add new tasks to the

---

Tip

A critical factor in business success is getting things done on time. To do so requires planning, scheduling, and schedule monitoring.

proper month's file whenever you learn of them.

2. On the first workday of the month, place the thirty-one-folder set behind the current month's divider. Then sort out that month's tasks by day, putting the proper tickler sheets in the folder for the day on which the task is to be done. You can add new sheets as the month goes on, or as new tasks come up. If a task is not done on the day it was tickled for, do not leave the sheet in the folder for that day. It will only be forgotten. Reassign a new date for the task and place the sheet in the proper folder.

3. Each evening, check the next day's tickler file and build those items into your boss's schedule or your own, as appropriate. If your boss is taking a trip, review the tickler file together for the days he will be gone to decide how those matters are to be handled.

4. For the year ahead you may want a set of folders by quarters. However, when you finish with January of this year, put that file at the end of the other eleven monthly files so it becomes January of the following year. Do the same with February, and so on through the year. You will need the quarter files only for items scheduled well into the year ahead.

5. If you postpone acting on a tickler sheet until it is no longer proper or reasonable to perform the task, destroy the sheet rather than continue to clutter up the tickler

system with it. This ensures that your tickler system is one you really use, not just a place to keep undone tasks off your desk and out of sight. Your tickler system should consist of informal notes to yourself and photocopies of other documents and correspondence; all originals are kept in the permanent file. That way, nothing of record is lost when you destroy a tickler sheet.

6. When you do the task, destroy the tickler sheet. It has served its purpose and you need not clutter up your files with tickler photocopies of originals already on file. Any correspondence that is a part of doing the task will be filed as part of the record.

Daily Reminder Notes

Keep a pad of plain notepaper on your desk for short notes to yourself. I have found 3" x 5" paper a convenient size, giving enough room for a fairly lengthy note, and handy for just a telephone number. Letter-size paper (8 1/2" x 11") is wasted when used for short reminder notes. Make notes of things to do during the day, or to discuss with your boss that day. If the task is to be done at a later time, put it into the tickler system. Don't trust your memory to remember to do something. Your attention can be easily and quickly transferred to so many things that it's hard to remember each little detail of something you thought of doing, said you would do, or were asked to do.

Tip

Don't get the reputation of being someone who says she will do something, but never does it or forgets about it.

Tip
Do not trust your memory to remember to do something. Write it down.

Write one item per sheet of notepaper. Line them up on the side of your desk so you can see them. If they get buried, they will be forgotten. Every time you take an action, throw away the note related to that task. Often your day will have flurries of hectic, high-pressure activity, followed by periods of relative quiet. Take advantage of the quieter times to do some tasks on your reminder notes. Part of your success as a secretary depends on the reputation you acquire in the company.   Don't get the reputation as someone who says she will do something, but never does it or forgets about it. Such a reputation will grow quickly if you make promises you fail to keep or are asked to do things you don't remember to do. Regular, faithful use of your calendar for reminding you about routine tasks, a working tickler system signaling nonroutine tasks, and a desk memo pad for little things that come up during the day will build the best reputation for dependability. The more people find out they can count on you, the more that reliability will be recognized and rewarded.

CHAPTER FIFTEEN

Memos

Memo writing is a communications form all its own. The dictionary defines a memorandum as a short note which serves as a reminder, written record, or communication. Most people say "memo" when speaking about a memorandum. Although the formal plural is "memoranda," most people refer to them in everyday office usage as "memos." The word "memorandum" is consistently used mainly as a heading for a preprinted or typed sheet of paper.

Direct Style for Memo Writing

In writing a memo, the normal style is to get right into the subject matter. The letter-writing conventions of a formal address and salutation are not part of memo-writing style. Memos skip the personal comments usually included in a business letter between friends to personalize the business contained in the letter. A memo can sometimes be less formal than a business letter to a stranger. If it is an *aide-mémoire*, the language is direct and formal. (An aide-mémoire is a notation of events and agreements for the record; its purpose is to recall to memory what happened.)

Types of Memos

Your boss may use memos for a number of reasons:

1. To remind someone to do something.
2. To explain to her boss (or others) why she did (or did not) do something.
3. To get a matter on the record in writing—an aide-mémoire. This may be a "memo to the file" so that your boss, or whoever handles the file in the future if she is transferred, will have this information available. A "memo to the file" is usually the summary of a telephone conversation or a thought about the situation. It may be a matter about which your boss anticipates some trouble or conflict in the future. By dictating a memo now, your boss protects herself against possible criticism or confrontation at some future time. Usually, this type of memo is dictated to someone, with several copies distributed, so the record is duly registered with a number of others.
4. To "blast" someone in the presence of others. "The presence of others" refers to those listed as receiving copies. This rather harsh use of a memo may backfire by start-

ing a memo barrage of charges, counter-charges, defenses, and positions taken. One of the dangers in using memos to conduct intraoffice warfare is the way it forces people to take firm public positions. Any movement away from a position is then seen as a victory for someone and a defeat for someone else.

5. To convey information. The facts can be about products, personnel, procedures, strategies, schedules, or any matter of interest to people in the company.

6. To make a proposal or a report. In memo form, a proposal or report is less formal than in report form. The proposed or reported issue may not be of a magnitude requiring a full-fledged proposal or report, though the matter still needs to be on paper.

7. To send an indirect message. The indirect message is conveyed by including the person for whom the message is really intended (but to whom it is not addressed) on the copy list. Your boss might not normally write directly to this person on this subject, but she wants to get a message to him. So she writes the memo to someone she would be expected to write it to, but "sneaks" the message to the person she really wants to reach by listing him as a copy. A second way to send an indirect message by memo is to copy someone who is a threat to the person to whom the memo is written. It is somewhat like saying, "You'd better pay attention to this because Mr. Montague now knows about it." In a sense, your boss is calling on Mr. Montague's power in the organization to back her up or to intimidate the person to whom the memo is addressed.

Forms for Writing Memos

Memos can be short—a single line; or long—several pages. They can be handwritten on a small desktop memo pad or typed on a printed memorandum form. Increasingly, they are written on a small desktop or portable computer and printed out by a dot-matrix printer on a role of tape paper. The part of the tape with the memo on it is then torn off and stapled to a regular memo sheet or letterhead sheet. This identifies the originator and ensures that the little piece of paper does not get lost. Or they can be written on a computer and entered into an electronic mail system. Other people in the system log in to see if they have received any memos. They can see the memo on their screen and get a hard-copy printout if they want one.

Memo Pads

If you have anything to say about the wording of small desktop memo pads, have yours say *Memo from Miss Anne Smith* or *Memo from Anne Smith* or just the company logo and *Anne Smith*. Please do not have them say *from the Desk of Anne Smith*, if you can help it. Does anyone enjoy receiving memos from someone's desk?

File Copies

You will have to exercise judgment about keeping copies of memos your boss originates. If it is a short, personal note confirming a lunch date, there is no reason to keep a copy beyond the date of the lunch. You already have a record of the date on your master calendar. If, however, it discusses a matter of substance, keep a copy in the file. It can be very important as part of an extended discussion on the matter, as memos and letters on a subject build up over several weeks, months, or even years.

Elements in a Memo

Date

Normally a memo follows a standard form. At the top, usually centered, is the word *Memorandum* or *MEMORANDUM*. The name of the company may be printed at the head of the paper, which is not generally of letterhead quality. The *Date* is placed on a line below the word *Memorandum*.

From/To

A *From/To* section is next. It makes little practical difference which is first. That's more a matter of house preference. Some organizations like *From* first, so the originator is readily identified. Others prefer *To* first, believing this gives the memo a more courteous flavor. Personally, I like *From* first. It gets right to business, saying who is writing the memo.

Subject

Next is the *Subject* section, providing a short description of the subject the memo covers. The *Subject* section is useful to focus attention on the point of the memo, and serves as a handle for filing purposes.

Body

The body of the memo follows. Many memo writers number their points—more often than they would in letter writing—to highlight their outline of thought. When people respond or comment on the memo, they can more easily refer to a statement in "item 4" than they can to "the fifth paragraph on page 2." Numbering the major points of a memo also makes it easier for recipients to follow the development of comments about the memo by making it possible for them to quickly locate points that are being discussed.

Copies

The final section of the memo contains a list of those who were sent copies of the memo, usually in alphabetical order. Some companies arrange this list by seniority, or at least put the president or chief executive officer at the top. In some firms, people who are not in the company but might get copies of the memo are listed at the head of the list, whereas company recipients are listed alphabetically. Depending on company style, the list is by last name only *(Henshaw)*, by initial and last name *(R. Henshaw)*, by social title and last name *(Miss Henshaw)*, by name and department *(Henshaw, Product Planning)*, or by first and last name *(Ruth Henshaw)*. Your boss will tell you the standard form to use in your company, even though she may give you only a list of last names. It is important that the copy list be complete. Apart from the times your boss is using copies for indirect messages, review the list in light of who has received copies of previous memos on the same subject. If someone has been left out, bring that to your boss's attention. The omission may have been merely an oversight, or it may have been deliberate. Only she knows which. Your job is to make sure no oversights occur.

Your Memos

Sometimes you will write a memo in your own name. For instance, your boss may ask you to make sure the rug is cleaned in her office before October 10 because she is having important visitors on that date. The rug cleaning is long overdue, and this visit provides a good reason for finally getting it

---

> **Tip**
>
> Memos can be short—a single line; or long—several pages.

done. You would send a memo to the person in charge of maintenance. It would be clear, but personal: clear because you are carrying out an order you want accomplished on time for everyone's sake; personal because you will continue to have to call on Maintenance to do things for you and your boss. You can telephone Maintenance to discuss the rug cleaning, but send the memo to confirm, and to get the matter in writing for the record in case of a problem in getting the job done on time.

Sample Memos

Here are some sample memos, using a variety of memo formats.

1. A memo to convey information and rearrange a schedule:

MEMORANDUM

March 15, 1999

From: Jane Jones

To: Al Twining

Subj: Schedule Change for Meeting with Delray, Inc.

The meeting with the development engineers at Delray has been postponed until April 18 at 10:30 A.M. The meeting is now scheduled to be held at their office in San Pablo.

The reason for the delay, so Delray tells me, is that they have had some trouble getting their TIRESIAS AI program and their knowledge engineer to sync on the needs of our customer. It seems that the inferences from the data are not making sense to the people at GT.

Let's have breakfast together at 7:30 A.M. on April 18 at Dempsey's on Route 161, review the situation as it is then, get our questions and requirements in order, and drive over together to Delray.

Copies: Bill Andrews
             Martha Belmont
             Ron Montague
             Tom Speare

---

2. A memo to report the results of a meeting, serving as an aide-mémoire, or to get the matter on the record for the future:

MEMORANDUM

April 19, 1999

From: Jane Jones

To: Ron Montague

Subj: Delray/GT problems

1. Sam Johnson at Delray called on March 14, asking that our meeting with them be postponed until mid-April. He reported that the GT people were not happy with the results from the prototype results of merging the TIRESIAS Artificial Intelligence program with the input provided by the knowledge engineer (Warren McDowell of Knowledge Systems, Inc.).

2. Al Twining and I had a meeting at Delray on April 18 with Sam Johnson, together with Dan Robbins of GT. The upshot of the day's discussion is that GT has lost confidence in Knowledge Systems's ability to debrief the experts at GT on special-guidance systems. GT believes that the TIRESIAS AI inferences are not sound because the expert knowledge base the inferences are constructed on are inaccurate. They do not believe Knowledge Systems is able to capture the subtleties in the expert knowledge GT's special-guidance people possess.

3. The meeting came to the following decisions:
    a. Knowledge Systems/GT/Delray/ourselves will find a knowledge systems expert to complement the work done so far by Knowledge Systems. GT will undertake the search for this expert.
    b. This expert will be contracted by Knowledge Systems. His costs will be absorbed by Knowledge Systems within the parameters of their budget arrangements with Delray.
    c. The expert must be on board by November 15. He will have two months to familiarize himself with the project and the current status of the project.

4. This restructuring will result in a possible four-month delay to our latest estimate of end-time completion date. GT can live with this, according to Dan Robbins.

5. The next full-scale review (Knowledge Systems/GT/Delray/us) will be at 10:30 A.M., Wednesday, May 15, in our conference room.

Copies: Sam Johnson (Delray)
          Warren McDowell (Knowledge Systems, Inc.)
          Dan Robbins (GT)
          Martha Belmont
          Tom Speare
          Al Twining

3. A memo to confirm a request for action and to get the request and agreement to act on the record:

MEMORANDUM

September 3, 1999

From: Nina Dow

To: Rich Turner

Subj: Cleaning Miss Smith's Carpet

This confirms our phone conversation earlier this morning about cleaning Miss Smith's carpet. She has asked that it be cleaned before October 6 so it will be dry by the 10th. You said you've got it scheduled for the night of October 4. Great! I know it'll look 1,000 percent better.

Thanks, Rich, for getting this done in time. Miss Smith asked me to pass along her thanks, too.

Copy: Miss Smith

CHAPTER SIXTEEN

Reports

Reports are part of business and government life. Your boss is assigned a task to research. He then has to make recommendations for approval and action. Or he may think of something he wants to initiate or an improvement he sees can be made. Research and a report is the way to bring the matter before others and get a decision.

People always say, "I want to see it on paper." They want a concise report they can use as the basis for rendering a judgment. They also want the report to serve as a part of a record, so they can refer back to it as the basis for later explaining their decision or for making further decisions. Report writing is mainly your boss's job. But preparing the report in a form that is clear, readable, and persuasive in appearance is yours. You may not have much input as to what it says, but you can influence how it looks. Some companies have standard report formats. If that is true of your company, study previous reports or reports presented by other executives (you can usually borrow a copy from another secretary) to find out how the company wants its reports to look. The elements that make up a standard report are:

1. Title page. This page is similar to the title page of a book. It gives essential information at a glance: the title of the report,

the name of the person or group that wrote the report, the date of the report, the depart-ment or company in which the report originated. Here is a sample title page:

A PROPOSAL FOR
THE ACQUISITION OF
MICROTECH DATA, INC.
Squantum, Massachusetts

October, 1999

prepared by

John R. Smith

Computronics International

---

2. Executive summary. Many reports provide a one-page summary of the report as the first page. Known as an "executive summary," it is prepared for busy executives who want to see at a single, brief reading what the report is all about and where it leads. Usually, the executive summary is written last, even though it is the first page to follow the title page. When writing it, your boss will be able to sense whether sections of his development of the report's main body are weak, and he may

decide to do some further writing or editing at that time.

The executive summary should contain the following sections: (1) purpose of the report; (2) main points discussed, listed numerically in outline form; (3) actions recommended, listed numerically and in order of importance. The executive summary is never more than a single page. It therefore may be necessary to type it single-spaced. Here is a sample executive summary:

A Proposal for the Acquisition of
MICROTECH DATA, INC.

Executive Summary

1. Purpose.

This proposal reports the results of a study concerning the possible acquisition of MICROTECH DATA, INC. by Computronics International to provide us with a software-product company that will augment our equipment line.

2. Our need for a software line.

In order to supply our customers with adequate software for our computer equipment, we need to either license or acquire an experienced software-product company, one with a full complement of programmers already in place and a proven track record of creating successful product. To develop our own internal software product division would be too costly and time-consuming. It is a field in which we do not have direct experience. We would lose valuable market time to learn about the field and attract the right personnel.

3. Licensing is unsatisfactory.

If we enter into a licensing agreement with a software firm, we are only one of several companies served. Our needs are such that we cannot afford to be just one of several; we need full-time attention to software development for our equipment and major marketing efforts.

4. Microtech Data, Inc.

Microtech Data, Inc., is the right company for us to acquire at this time. Its history, personnel on hand, marketing know-how, and present financial condition are a good blend for immediate acquisition.

5. Recommendation.

That we proceed to negotiate acquisition of Microtech Data, Inc., with a view to completed takeover no later than December 12, 1999.

As a result of reading the executive summary, an executive who receives a copy of the report may react in any one of a number of ways:

a. He may decide the report contains information only for him. The executive summary gives him enough information for his purposes, and he has the report filed in case he ever needs to refer to it again.

b. The executive decides he is concerned about the subject under discussion, so he reads the entire report in great detail to fill himself in on all the supporting material backing up the executive summary. He may send for more information to obtain further support, or challenge some information or the conclusions your boss has drawn from the data.

c. The executive has to make a decision based on the material in the report. He not only reads it in detail, but calls your boss for further consultation about various points your boss made and her recommendations for action. He assigns some further research on one or two points to your boss before he (the senior executive) presents the matter to a committee. The executive summary, however, is the skeleton around which he structures his presentation and recommendations.

3. The main body of the report. The report is usually divided into sections, based on an overall outline. Sections can include: background (introductory material that puts the report into perspective); purpose (what the report is designed to achieve); definition of terms (if technical words are used in the report, a glossary of these terms early in the report helps the reader understand the words to mean the same thing the writer intends); points in the outline (main sections that describe research done, facts uncovered, areas investigated, and the like); and recommended or required actions (depending on whether the report is going up the chain of authority for consideration or down the chain for implementation). It is important in a report to have enough divisions of the material at logical stopping points, and to have them labeled. This gives the reader guideposts throughout the report so he can know what he is looking at, where he has been, and where he is going. These guideposts are called "heads." Normally, a report will have two levels of heads (*A* and *B* heads); it might have as many as four (*A*, *B*, *C*, and *D* heads). To help the reader know which is which and how they relate to each other, it is useful for each type of head to look different typographically.

A heads can be all caps, flush left, with two line spaces above and one line space below. If there is an outline number or letter, that should be used as part of the *A* head.

1. BACKGROUND

This is the general appearance of an *A* head with an outline number. The main points in a report are *A*-head titles. *B* heads can be upper- and lowercase, flush left, one line space above and one line space below. *B* heads are used for divisions of thought and text within a main point and are subordinate to the *A* head.

a. Company Experience to the Present

This is the general appearance of a *B* head with an outline letter. *B* heads are subsections of material in a main section. Usually, there are two or more *B* heads under a single *A* head if the material in the *A*-head section is divided into smaller sections. *C* heads can be upper- and lowercase, beginning with an indentation from the left margin, one line space above and one line space below. *C* heads are used for subsections within a *B*-head section.

    i. Company Experience: 1965–1986

This is the general appearance of a *C* head. In such a development of material, a second *C* head might carry the historical analysis further:

    ii. Company Experience: 1987–1999

D heads can be upper- and lowercase, underlined, or italics (if you have a word processor or an italics typing element for your typewriter), beginning with an indentation from the left margin, one line space above and one line space below. *D* heads are seldom used, since they are subsections of subsections of subsections. Unless the report is carefully structured and very complex, with a clear outline, the significance of *D* heads can readily be overlooked by the casual reader.

    (a) Experience: 1976–1999—Atlanta
    (b) Experience: 1976–1999—Houston
    (c) Experience: 1976–1999—Denver

These three *D* heads suggest how a report might break down an analysis in some detail, based on regional centers or marketing centers or product lines, depending on the nature of the company and the purpose of the report.

4. Contents. After the report is completed, with page numbers, prepare a table of contents, using the *A*-, *B*-, *C*-, and *D*-head titles as the titles in the table of contents. Indent each level of heads. The page number can follow each entry by three spaces, or can be flush right at the end of the entry. If the entry is two or more lines, the page number should be on the last line of the entry. A sample contents page can be seen on page 111. The contents page is usually placed immediately after the executive summary, or after the title page if there is no executive summary.

If the final report is typed single-spaced, it may appear too crowded unless frequent heads break up the feeling of close-typed, wall-to-wall copy. If it is typed double-spaced, it may appear too open and too long for easy reading since it takes up so many sheets of paper. Sometimes the best solution is to use one-and-a-half-line spacing. This is easy to read and more condensed than double spacing. Any draft copies of a report should be typed double-spaced—or even triple-spaced if your equipment has that option—so your boss can easily edit, adjust, rewrite, and add. In today's office, a report that will require text manipulation and change before the final copy is prepared should be entered into a word-processing system. If you do not have one yourself, have your boss make arrangements with the appropriate people in the company so that versions of the report are done on a word processor. This not only saves much retyping, but insures that new errors are not continually introduced into the report during the process of constant retyping. A report should have numbered pages. The numbers can be placed at the center top or bottom of each page. Or they can be flushed to the right at the top, with the name of the report or the name of the section of the report:

TOWN OF SQUANTUM: Water Resources 2

Sample Contents Page of a Report

1. BACKGROUND: OUR NEED FOR A SOFTWARE DIVISION OR SUBSIDIARY — 1

2. DEVELOP OUR OWN — 3
   a. Experience Required — 3
   b. Cost Required — 4
   c. Time Required — 6

3. LICENSE SOFTWARE FROM EXISTING SOFTWARE COMPANY — 8
   a. Royalties and Contracts — 8
   b. Competing Claims of Other Clients — 11
   c. Competing Marketing Image — 15

4. ACQUIRE SOFTWARE COMPANY — 17
   a. Where to Position in Structure — 17
   b. How to Coordinate Sales Impact — 19
   c. Optimum Timing — 22

5. MICROTECH DATA, INC. — 25
   a. History — 25
   b. Present Condition — 28
      i. Finances — 28
      ii. Personnel — 31
      iii. Software Know-how — 34
      iv. Inventory — 35
      v. Location — 39

6. ACQUISITION OF MICROTECH DATA, INC. — 40
   a. Terms — 40
   b. Timing — 42
   c. Trade and Public Announcement — 44

On the first page of the report, the page number is often centered at the bottom of the page, even though all the following pages have the numbers in the upper right-hand corner. Most word-processing systems can save you time with automatic page numbering. Some can also prepare a table of contents. Check your manual for details.

To make the most professional impression, the report should be placed in a presentation folder. These are sometimes folders with three-hole clasps. Sometimes a plastic gripper is placed along the left-hand side of the folder, or a plastic comb binding can be used to dress up the presentation and insure the report receives extra attention. If a report is worth the executive time to prepare and the secretarial time to produce, it can be worth a few more cents to call attention to its importance by dressing it in a presentation folder.

CHAPTER SEVENTEEN

Financial Statements

Depending on your boss's role in the company, you may have to type financial statements from time to time. If you have a word processor or have access to one, these statements are far easier to prepare. Mistakes are easier to correct in word processing, and it is impossible to get every figure absolutely right in a complex financial statement. An even greater benefit of word-processing financial statements is the ability to retain the format and copy data without having to retype it (thus avoiding introducing new typos while retyping). Usually in a financial statement, last year's figures for the same period are shown alongside this year's figures. It is easy on a word-processing system to make "this year's" figures into "last year's" figures when you add a new set of "this year's" figures, provided you kept the diskette for financial statements. You delete the old figures, move the present figures for this year into the last year's column, and add this year's new figures. In word processing, you retain the overall format and one-half of the figures you need; you have only to add the new figures for the period being reported. Financial statements are usually prepared quarterly. Annual figures are included in the company's annual report.

Usually financial statements have two sections. One is the "profit-and-loss" or "income-and-expenditure" summary of monies received and monies spent during the period being reported. The second is a "balance sheet," or statement of present

Statement of Consolidated Income

	This year	Last year	Increase Decrease
	(In Thousands)		
Net Sales	$1,792,938	$1,637,482	$155,456
Cost of Goods Sold	1,324,595	1,214,561	110,034
Gross Profit	468,343	422,921	45,422
Less:			
Selling and administrative expenses .	179,611	162,779	16,832
Research, development, patent, and			
engineering expenses	86,281	84,224	2,057
	265,892	247,003	18,889
Operating Profit	202,451	175,918	26,533
Income Charges—Net	11,519	10,445	1,074
Income Before Income Taxes	190,932	165,473	25,459
Provision for Income Taxes:			
Current	83,908	70,238	13,670
Deferred (credit)	(1,801)	(3,462)	1,661
	82,107	66,776	15,331
Income Before Extraordinary Item	108,825	98,697	10,128
Extraordinary Gain on Sale of Investment, Less Applicable Income Tax of $2,131,000		6,394	6,394
Net Income	$ 108,825	$ 105,091	$ 3,734

Consolidated Balance Sheet

December 31	This year	Last year
Assets		
Current assets		
Cash	$ 12,622,000	$ 10,623,000
Marketable securities, at cost which approximates market value...	1,793,000	1,142,000
Accounts receivable, less reserve:		
This year, $778,000; Last year, $616,000	52,873,000	38,313,000
Inventories	47,461,000	43,410,000
Other current assets and prepayments	6,729,000	3,114,000
Total current assets	121,478,000	96,602,000
Capital assets	82,194,000	73,928,000
Patents and goodwill, less amortization	2,207,000	2,763,000
Other assets	2,225,000	1,713,000
Total assets	$208,104,000	$175,006,000
Liabilities and stockholder's equity		
Current liabilities		
Accounts payable	$ 24,973,000	$ 18,828,000
Income taxes payable.	7,498,000	886,000
Notes payable and current portion of long-term debt	6,210,000	15,116,000
Advance billings	17,876,000	15,842,000
Total current liabilities	56,557,000	50,672,000
Deferred taxes on income	5,344,000	6,156,000
Long-term debt	34,453,000	15,724,000
Total liabilities	96,354,000	72,552,000
Stockholders' equity		
4% convertible cumulative preferred stock, $50 par value	12,000,000	12,000,000
Common stock, $2 par value.	11,973,000	11,922,000
Capital in excess of par value	19,743,000	18,517,000
Retained earnings	68,034,000	60,015,000
Total stockholders' equity	111,750,000	102,454,000
Total liabilities and stockholders' equity	$208,104,000	$175,006,000

worth. The profit and loss, usually abbreviated *P/L*, is a historical record over a period of time. The balance sheet is a kind of snapshot of total worth at the moment the picture is taken. Reporting can be quarterly or annual (three- and twelve-month) periods. In some summaries, the history may go back longer than the same period last year if long-term trends are being studied or presented. A sample of each kind of financial statement follows. Your company's financial statements will differ somewhat in that accounting practices may differ and the nature of your company's business will call for different categories. But, by and large, the same general kinds of categories will appear. A *P/L* statement gives a recording of the sources of income to the company, the kinds of expenditures made, and whether there was overall profit or loss for the reporting period. On page 114 is a *P/L* statement, showing last year, this year, and the amount of increase or decrease.

The balance sheet gives a summary of assets (things or money the company has or money owed to the company), liabilities (obligations the company has to others), and net worth (the difference between the assets and the liabilities). If, for instance, a company has assets of over $100,000 but owes $35,000, the net worth of the company is $65,000. Sometimes the net worth is called stockholders' or owners' equity, meaning how much the company would be worth to them after all the bills are paid. Page 115 has a sample balance sheet.

My purpose in showing you these forms is not to teach accounting or how to read a financial statement. (You may want to learn how to read a financial statement, so you can recognize when your company is in trouble and you should begin looking elsewhere, but that is a by-product of working at preparing these statements.) This section of *Secretarial Practice Made Simple* is simply to alert you to the general appearance of these statements and their general contents. Because they summarize your company's activity—and disclose whether the company has made any money—they are of great interest to company executives, board members, stockholders, and the general financial public. Accuracy and a pleasing appearance are essential in a company's financial statements.

CHAPTER EIGHTEEN

Meetings

If your boss is responsible for conducting committee meetings, part of your work will be to assist him with preparation and follow-up for these meetings. Your responsibilities may include physical arrangements for the meeting itself, depending on where it is held.

Agenda

Preparation for a meeting requires determining an agenda—the topics to be considered—and a list of who should attend the meeting. For an established committee, attendees include members of the committee, any specially invited guests or experts, and any company staff who normally or by special invitation sit in on this committee.

You will have a list of the committee members and regular staff attendees. Your boss will add special guests and other company staff who should be at this meeting.

Once your boss sets the agenda and the list of attendees, you should send out an announcement of the meeting, with a copy of the agenda. The announcement should include the date, time, and place of the meeting, plus the address and telephone number to call or write to decline or confirm attendance. Confirmation of attendance is important if food is to be served or if the meeting is to be held at a location requiring hotel reservations. The meeting notice and agenda should be sent sufficiently ahead of the meeting date so that everyone feels he has been given a fair chance to consider the

---

Tip

To prepare for a meeting, an agenda—or list of topics to be considered—has to be set down.

---

topics and prepare for the meeting. Two weeks is usually considered sufficient. For some meetings, such as stockholders' meetings, you are legally required to inform those invited a specific number of days before the meeting.

Reports and Financial Statements

Certain items on the agenda may call for reports or financial statements to be presented at the meeting for discussion. Part of your boss's responsibility for the meeting is to see that these reports and financial statements or statistical summaries are prepared in advance, and presented in handout or audiovisual form at the meeting. Part of your job will be to put reports and statements in the form he wishes, or to make sure they are properly prepared.

As formal company documents, these reports will follow a standard format. They are kept with the records of the work of that committee and as part of the company archives. Care in their preparation is essential. Give yourself adequate time to proofread them so that neither you nor your boss is embarrassed by a committee member pointing out typos. If your financial reports are not computer printouts, be sure to add each column of figures. Otherwise, some committee member playing mental games during the meeting may add the columns and catch your boss in an arithmetic error, thus clouding his credibility on the points he is trying to make.

Physical Arrangements

You need to insure the physical arrangements are fully made for the meeting. The best way to insure that everything is planned is to develop a checklist you run through for each meeting. Every once in a while something will come up that you had not foreseen. Even though you cannot provide for it at that particular meeting, add the item to your meeting checklist to make sure it is not a problem again.

A Checklist for a Meeting at the Company

A meeting checklist should contain the following items, plus others required by your boss, your special circumstances, and your experience:

1. Reserve the meeting room.
2. Personally check the room before the meeting to make sure:
   a. Enough chairs are on hand.
   b. The room is clean.
   c. Water and glasses are at convenient locations on the table.
   d. Notepads and pencils are at each seat.
   e. Sufficient ashtrays are on the table.
   f. The room is at the right temperature.
   g. Name cards are placed, if desired.
   h. Required audiovisual equipment is on hand and working.
   i. A podium is on hand, if desired, with a working microphone or sound system.

3. Verify that security and receptionists know the meeting is scheduled and where to direct people who come from outside the company.

4. Confirm catering and serving arrangements, if food is part of the meeting schedule—whether you've planned lunch, a coffee break with pastry, or afternoon drinks.

5. Check that any exhibits to be passed around during the meeting are on hand.

Additional Items To Check for a Meeting Outside the Company

If the meeting is held at a hotel or conference center, other complications are possible. Your meeting checklist should include:

6. Transportation to and from the location.

7. Room reservations for each person staying over, including who will share rooms if single accommodations are not company policy.

8. Meal arrangements, including menu selection for any meal in a private dining room.

9. Payment arrangements, permitting those attending to sign for room and meal charges.

10. Posting of meeting schedule and location in a central location.

11. Return to your office of unused or permanent materials.

When your boss is responsible for arranging or running the meeting, you will need to review this checklist with him to make some of the items more specific. Give him a typed copy of the final checklist, with all details noted, so he will have a ready answer if asked about any detail. He will know what was not anticipated if something unexpected happens. His on-the-spot decision-making will be better when he sees clearly all the arrangements that were made during the planning of the meeting.

If You Attend the Meeting

If you attend the meeting, whether in the company or outside, part of your responsibility is seeing that all runs smoothly according to plan. The reason for a meeting is the accomplishment of the business on the agenda. Attendees are there to concentrate on the business at hand, not on the physical arrangements, which should require no attention from meeting participants.

Minutes of the Meeting

During a meeting, some record usually must be kept. The nature of these minutes or proceedings varies from company to company and meeting to meeting. If your boss asks you to "take minutes," clarify beforehand how extensive a record he wants. Perhaps the best way at first—until you come to a mutual understanding of what is needed—is to make notes around the topics listed on the agenda. They will serve as a basis for him to dictate a record of the meeting. Your notations will act as reminders of what was discussed. A lot of ex-

---

Tip

Drop a short note of thanks to key people whose help made the meeting run smoothly.

> **Tip**
>
> When the immediate post-meeting tasks are completed, review all the arrangements with your boss to see how the next meeting can be even better.

changes will probably go unreported, being either repetitious or irrelevant. Your boss will have a good sense of what to retain from the discussion as he reviews your "memory jogger" notes.

If a formal resolution is passed, record it word for word at the meeting. Time is often spent at meetings agreeing on exact wording; attendees will be grateful when you persist in making sure those exact words are in your notes.

For note-taking at a meeting, shorthand can be useful. However, it is not essential. You can develop your own abbreviation system. Apart from formal resolutions, you generally do not need verbatim accounts or records. You will have to listen and summarize the gist of what is said. A business meeting is not a court of law in which a transcriber has to take down every hem and haw as well as every word. The report or minutes of a meeting is a general record of what took place; this record often becomes a point of reference for new directions and improved performance by company employees.

Follow-Up After the Meeting

The final matter to handle after the meeting, once the record has been prepared, is to send out any material promised to those who attended. Participants may have decided that certain other executives in the company should receive a copy of the proceedings or of other material discussed

during the meeting. This offers them a chance to get in touch with your boss if they feel some important matter was left out or not quite correctly recorded. It will also inform executives in the company of what took place, even though they did not attend. Your boss will determine who is on the "for your information" list to receive a copy of the proceedings.

Always drop a short note of thanks to key people whose help made the meeting run smoothly. Some of these notes should be in your boss's name; others can be in yours. People who feel appreciated for having done their job well will try even harder the next time. Those whose hard work is taken for granted grow less and less committed as time goes on.

The Next Meeting

When the immediate post-meeting tasks are completed, review all the arrangements with your boss to see how the next meeting can be even better. Make your checklist the agenda for your review, and develop a modified checklist for next time, based on your experience with the meeting just past. The sole business of some consulting firms is arranging meetings for companies. Read their books and announcements for hints; keep your eyes open for new ideas as you attend meetings conducted by others. Thorough and smooth meeting arranging is an excellent skill for career advancement.

CHAPTER NINETEEN

Filing

"Please bring the file on the Johnson account when you come." "The file" is an almost magical incantation in the office. When a detail is forgotten, an agreement needs to be reviewed, or questions arise about a matter, "the file" is searched to find the answer.

The file contains pieces of paper: copies of incoming and outgoing correspondence, copies of orders, statements of accounts, shipping documents, copies of memos, handwritten notes summarizing a telephone conversation, memos to the file. It serves as a running record of relationships, agreements, and controversies with other parties. If a critical piece is missing—or was never created—the file cannot provide the needed answer. When everything is there, the file provides background for making the next decision about an ongoing business relationship.

The Keeper of the File

The file reflects activity between your boss and her business colleagues. As its keeper, you determine what goes in. It's your responsibility if crucial papers are missing. You have to be able to put your hands on any file immediately and know where a file is at any moment—on your boss's desk, in her briefcase, at her home, on your desk, in the drawer, on the typist's desk. And you have to know how this file relates to others on similar subjects.

The File as an Ongoing Record

Very seldom in a career does a secretary have the job of creating a system of files. Many different filing systems exist, each with its own benefits and disadvantages. Since you usually inherit an ongoing filing system, *Secretarial Practice Made Simple* does not discuss possible filing systems you might install if you had the opportunity. (Only once in four decades of office work did I have an opportunity to set up files the way I thought they should be—when I established my own company. Even then my partner got into the act in ways I found less than perfect. *B.H.*) So you will usually work with a filing system that has had many secretaries and bosses, sometimes benefiting and other times suffering from them, and that will undoubtedly outlast both you and your boss in that department.

As you maintain your files, keep in mind those who will follow you. Will they be able to find what they are looking for? It is no compliment to be known as the only person who can find something in your files. Even your boss may have to look for something when you are ill or she is working on a weekend.

Learn the Files

Read each file as you need it. Scan other files in the early days on the job, before you are so busy that you do not have the leisure to browse through them. When you add to one, see how what you insert relates to what occurred before. When correspondence comes in and you pull the file to send to your boss with the newly arrived letter, glance through the file to get a feeling for the subject and people involved.

Respect the Files

At first, put more into the file than not. In time, you will develop a feel for what is significant and should be kept and what is trivial and need not be filed. But when you begin working with a file, err on the side of retaining too much. You can always clean out the trivia at a later time, but you can never reconstruct data that was thrown away hastily.

Introduce Any Changes to the Files Slowly and Cautiously

The system has worked somehow until now. Your concept of how files should be organized may be superficially sound, but have serious flaws for the future. Make changes in filing only after you have been in the job long enough to know your modifications to the system will be true improvements, bringing those who inherit your files a better system than the one you found. Keep your changes minor, improving but not radically restructuring the files. Major

---

Tip

Usually you have to work with a filing system that has had many secretaries and bosses—sometimes benefiting and other times suffering from them—and that will undoubtedly outlast both you and your boss.

Tip

It is not a compliment to be known as the only person who can find something in your files.

---

change to a filing system is a massive task that will keep you from other activities for months. Is the end result of all that time and effort and distraction from other activity worth it? Usually not.

Housekeeping

Do "housekeeping" on the files, but only after you know what is important. It takes several months on the job to gain a perspective on the pieces of paper that make up a file. After you have served your apprenticeship, review each file as you need it and throw away trivia that has accumulated. Memos and letters about meeting dates long past need no longer take up file space. If Accounting keeps records of outdated information found in your file, it can be tossed out. But anything that looks as though it has any long-term value should be kept. You may decide months from now, when you next pull the file and review its contents, that a particular piece of paper can go, but better to make that decision later than sooner. The balance to be struck is somewhere between being a pack rat, who collects and stores everything, and a careless destroyer of information that will have value in the years ahead. The key is to save too much at the beginning and throw much of it out during later reviews of the file.

Originals of Contracts and Agreements

Originals of contracts and formal agreements are best saved in a secure alternative filing location or a separate folder, but keep a copy of the original in the working file with a notation of where the original is kept. The originals are legal documents, often of considerable worth to the company and very difficult, if not impossible, to duplicate if lost. Staple copies of such documents to the file folder so that even a copy will not be accidentally discarded.

Your boss may need copies of financial reports and records sent from Accounting or the treasurer's office only as long as they are useful management tools for her. The firm's official copies are maintained elsewhere in the company. Work out with your boss an estimate of how long she typically needs these reports in her own work. Keep them at least that long—perhaps a quarter longer—and then throw them out. If she ever needs a copy a year or two later, she can request one from the originating office.

Confidential Information

If you throw away confidential information as you maintain the files, use a shredder or tear the material into two or four pieces. Many companies view financial records as confidential, so those documents should not be thrown undestroyed into the trash. Your boss can guide you regarding company policy on what is confidential and how those records are to be destroyed when no longer needed.

Space for Files

Files and file maintenance cost money. The files themselves take space—valuable space that the company pays for by the square foot each year. Additional file drawers are expensive. A file clerk's time or your efforts to keep the files current and to access them is much more costly now than it was years ago. Your efforts to control the size and growth of the files is of great value to the company.

Microfilming Files

In many companies, the expense of space for growing files is so great that they have adopted the policy of microfilming them. The file is photographed and reduced to the size of a large postage stamp. It can be read only with an enlarging device; often photocopies can be made so you or your boss can have a hard copy. These miniature copies are either on a roll of film or assembled on a card called a microfiche. Valuable original documents are preserved; normal file

contents are microfilmed and kept at a central repository or library; this year's working file is maintained by you in your office. You may send down an old file every so often for microfilming.

If you are ever in an office while it converts to microfilming, you will go through a nightmarish year while your older files are processed. If, however, you come into an office where microfilming is standard practice, you have only to learn the pattern and adapt to it.

Your boss cannot retrieve microfilmed files as readily as she can your current file. It takes time for the file archivist to locate the microfilm, copy what is needed, and send it to you. Depending on the situation and the urgency, it may take hours or weeks.

Files and the File Clerk

You may do your own filing or have a file clerk working for you. That file clerk may work full-time for you or serve several secretaries from a centralized file area. Never become so dependent on a file clerk that you are paralyzed when he is sick or on vacation. You should be able to find your way around your own files when the file clerk is busy on some other assignment. Don't let your file clerk take over your files; remember that this employee works for you. Let him know that you see what he does about the files, and you will be able to keep control

Tip

Make changes in files only after you have been in the job long enough to know your modifications to the system will be a true improvement.

of his work. A slipshod file clerk can damage you and your boss very quickly.

Cross-Referencing Files

Cross-reference filing may sound impressive in books about filing, but often results in more confusion and greater loss of effective working time than in any positive gains. It is much easier to photocopy a document and put a copy in each place you think it belongs—indicating on the copy where the master is filed. (Remember to remove copies when they are no longer needed).

Filing Suggestions

Some standard filing suggestions are worth repeating; they are sound and based on proven practice:

1. File correspondence files alphabetically, with the most recent date on top.

2. File subject files according to a pattern that makes good sense in your office, breaking a subject into sub-categories only when you find good reason to do so.

3. Staple pieces of related correspondence together. Do not use paper clips to hold paper together.

4. File the most recent papers on top, and work backward through time to the bottom of the file.

5. If someone takes (or is sent) part of a file, drop in a piece of paper with a brief description of what was sent, when, and to whom. You never know when you might need to track it down.

No file is ever in perfect condition, as each one is always in a state of change. Remember that files exist for the sake of the job; employees do not exist to maintain files. Make the files produce for you and your boss. You will learn what they can do for you as the job goes on. For the files to produce what you want when you want it requires your careful and consistent attention, but the end result of an easy, working filing system is a better and easier job for you.

Be a pragmatist about your files, not a perfectionist. Devote as much attention to them as they need, but no more. Use your extra time for career development in other aspects of your job.

CHAPTER TWENTY

The Automated Office

As we near the twenty-first century, the proliferation of computers and automated machines in the workplace will continue. The growing trend toward personal computers has already made the standard electronic typewriter obsolete. Expanding technologies like voice mail are quickly outdating older forms of communication.

In the 1990s, many offices will install new kinds of computer equipment. Learning to use these machines effectively will make your work more efficient and pleasant. More importantly, it will add valuable and marketable skills to your work experience.

Records Management

You can choose to organize the information you save on your computer disks in many ways. Deciding factors include: how many people you prepare documents for, what type of industry you are in, how many customers you handle, and whether you save documents to a hard- or floppy-disk drive.

The ability to locate stored information quickly is crucial to satisfactory job performance, so setting up a system and using it becomes very important. In some firms, a standardized method of naming, saving, and backing up documents is used. If your workplace has one, learn the system thoroughly and do not deviate. If your firm has this type of system, you'll probably find a word-processing department and/or a "Help" line to call for information and assistance. Use these resources whenever you have a question—don't be shy; that's why they exist.

You may inherit a previous secretary's system, which you can choose to use or change. Either way, be sure you understand the system so that you can find the documents she created.

Ways to name a document include:

1. Numerical log. Assign a chronological number to each new document and enter the vital information into a log you keep handy at your desk. If you use this method, it is wise to include the document number somewhere in the document, such as the bottom left or top right corner.

2. Author's name. Use a separate disk for each person you do work for, and use another document (such as subject or recipient) to name each document on that disk.

3. Client or project name. Use the same method as in *Author's name* (Item 2 above).

The most logical approach is to choose a system which mirrors the one you use for paper files in the office. In this way, information can be stored and retrieved consistently by all users.

You may want to take advantage of a file management software program, which can print out lists of the files you have saved to disk or tape. These can serve as a directory. Some software programs will also print out labels to attach directly to your disk. Your current software program may have a similar feature, so do some research or ask your computer consultant. Different software packages have individual ways of organizing and listing files. You may find that your program dictates the way you store information. Sometimes the best choice is to simply keep a handwritten log or directory in a notebook.

The most common way to group information is by using a separate floppy disk or path—if you always save to your hard drive—for each author or by subject matter. Then within that broader category each document is named (as described above). It's most important to be consistent: always name documents in the same way, and communicate your method so that other people can find documents in your absence. Give your boss a memo explaining your method and keep a copy near the computer to avoid confusion.

Editing

Because computers and word processors allow for easier revisions than typewriters, you will find that each document you work on often goes through numerous changes, variations, and developments. You may also find yourself doing editorial work on the documents that your boss creates, or tailoring form letters and documents to specific situations.

Two types of software can assist you in these tasks: spelling checkers (some even have a thesaurus to provide synonyms) and grammar checkers. When you use these programs, they review the document you were working on, highlight potential problems, and suggest corrections which you may accept or reject.

To conserve paper, get into the habit of proofreading each document you create on the computer before printing it out.

Computer Back-Up Procedures

Accidents happen. That's why it is crucial to periodically back up the information you store on your computer system by making a copy. Whether you have a hard or floppy disk, files will occasionally disappear. Power surges, electrical failure, a damaged disk, or a spilled liquid are the major problems, but you can overcome them. Having a back-up copy will save you hours of work if any of these things ever happen in your office.

Your company may have a procedure which you are required to follow. If so, do it and consider that requirement the bare minimum. Some people back up each document as it is created, and again after each revision. Others back up all their work at the end of the day, week, or month. Whatever method you use—and we strongly suggest you back up frequently—be sure to schedule enough time. The process can be long and tedious, and easy to postpone.

The Myth of the "Paperless Office"

In the early days of automation, experts predicted that offices would soon become "paperless." In theory, everything would be stored on disk or tape, media which take up far less space than "hard copy" or paper records. Unfortunately, most offices do not have the type of computer system which allows employees access to records by a method they can use easily. As a result, most offices now save all documents on disk or tape in addition to having the traditional paper files. If you are ever involved in the transition from typewriter to computer, you may be surprised to discover you now actu-ally have twice as many documents to keep track of as before.

Monitoring Information on Disks

Periodically checking the documents stored on disks serves two useful functions. The primary reason for tracking the stored documents is basic housekeeping. When you review a disk's contents, you can search for things that can be deleted, moved to a better location, or duplicated if appropriate. Secondarily, you will want to routinely check the amount of storage space available on your disks. In this way, you always know there will be enough space to store the documents you are creating.

Working with LANs

A recent trend is to link personal comput-ers together in a system called a LAN: local-area network. If your workstation includes a computer which is part of a LAN, you will, in effect, be sharing software, document storage, and some computer hardware components (perhaps a printer or modem) with other people.

The advantage of using a LAN is that it is easier to share and exchange information between computers. The disadvantage is that you may have to wait to use documents or certain functions if someone else is using the system at the same time.

Workstations with Shared Equipment

If you work on a LAN or share a com-puter, printer, or other automated equip-ment with other office staff, you will want to exercise good judgment in using these devices. Think ahead. Do your best to prioritize your work and plan it so that shared equipment will not become a problem in meeting deadlines. You will also want to be assertive about scheduling your usage of these machines both for your own needs and in working with other people to meet their deadlines. Communication is the most important thing, so try to inform people when you are beginning a large project. Be willing to accommodate other people's requests, and cooperate with them to insure that you have the use of shared equipment when your own work requires it.

The Versatile Modem

Modems are attached to computers to allow them to communicate and share information. Basically, modems use phone lines to send information. In combination with the computer and communications software, the modem allows the computer user to compose a document, call up a location, and send or receive information. Modems make it possible for computer users to have access to massive amounts of current information, as well as to communicate with other computer users and fax machines.

Here are some common applications: in law firms modems are used with special software to do research on legal matters. In financial companies, modems keep track of minute by minute developments in the financial community. In worldwide corporations, modems send and receive interoffice mail twenty-four hours a day and send information to all offices simultaneously. When used properly, modems allow you to send and retrieve information quickly and inexpensively.

Sending

With your modem and appropriate software you can send information to individuals or to other locations. This process is known as electronic communication. Procedures differ, depending on the equipment and software, but the basic steps are similar. You create a document, with either your normal word-processing program or your communications program, and then send it via modem to another location where it will be received by another computer terminal or printer. Some programs and services allow you to send documents directly from your personal computer to a facsimile machine.

Many large companies have an electronic communications network tailored to their exclusive use. Small businesses may subscribe to large communications networks (such as Compuserve) to send information. Whatever method is used, you will probably be surprised at how easy and fast these systems are once you learn how they work.

Receiving

Because electronic communication stores information in a central area, anyone can theoretically send and receive messages. To protect confidential documents, a password or code is normally assigned to each user in a system. Many systems additionally require users to verify or change their codes periodically. You will probably have access to both your own and your boss's codes. Be sure to write them down in a safe place if you can't memorize them.

When you receive information, you normally "sign on" or call up the system with your modem and then check your "mailbox" to see if anything has been sent to you.

If you have something waiting, you then "download" it or transfer the information from the communications system to your own computer. Depending on the specific system you use, you can save the information, print it out, or delete it after reading. Many systems charge by time usage, and since you tie up a telephone line when using a modem, it is usually most efficient if you download information and save it on a disk. Then you can sign off the system and stop the charges and phone usage while you work with the documents and information you have been sent.

Coping with Today's Faster Pace

Because today's office is becoming more and more automated and the emphasis is placed on information, the daily pace can be very fast. The workload may sometimes appear overwhelming. You will want to use your time management and communications skills to help you handle your assignments.

Time Management

Many theories, books, tapes, and classes are available on time management. Most of them are good and can be helpful. Find out what is available to you and study time management in order to help yourself. Many companies will pay for this training if they do not offer it in-house, as good time management benefits everyone.

You may find it useful to work closely with your boss if she does not manage time well, since the way she works has a strong impact on your own activities. Helping her to structure her workload makes your day easier.

Communication with Your Manager

Keep your manager up-to-date about the assignments you are currently handling, and check with her to make sure you agree on priority items and deadlines. Know your abilities and limitations and keep your manager informed when you think you will not be able to meet a deadline, or feel the quality of your work is suffering because of time limitations. Work with your boss in delegating assignments to insure that projects are completed on time.

Lighting and Office Furniture

Many office managers are becoming more aware of the need to adapt furniture and lighting for the new equipment now in use. This has led to special heights in desks, tables, and chairs, as well as furniture designed specifically to provide support and good posture for the user. This new trend in design is known as "ergonomics." Many people believe that using furniture created for the automated office increases productivity and decreases sick days taken by employees because of the discomfort and back pain caused by poor posture at workstations. If your furniture is uncomfortable, you may want to replace it with pieces designed for the equipment you use.

Another element to consider is lighting. If you use a computer, you may find that the glare from windows and overhead light causes eyestrain. Computer filters are the best way to alleviate this problem. These tinted glass (or plastic) covers fit over your computer screen to reduce glare and blurred vision. Although they can be costly (some filters run as high as fifty dollars or more), they are becoming increasingly popular.

Your computer dealer will be able to tell you more about pricing and the different kinds of filters available.

If a filter is not a viable option, there are other ways you can alleviate glare. Try to rearrange your computer or desk so that you are more comfortable, or use "task lighting"—a lamp instead of overhead fluorescent bulbs—if possible. Another possibility, if your office has fluorescent fixtures, is to use full-spectrum bulbs (such as Vita-lite) or mix cool and warm fluorescent bulbs to ease eyestrain.

Automated Postage Meters

Most large firms have a centralized mail department, and the secretary is responsible only for addressing mail and getting it to the mail room for postage and delivery. However, at a small or midsize company, you will probably be using a postage meter yourself. Several manufacturers make postage meters, which are generally small, but quite noisy. They are normally kept wherever the photocopier and other machines are found.

To use the postage meter, you will need to first weigh the envelope or package to be sent, then calculate the correct amount of postage. Enter the correct dollar amount of the required postage. Then print a sticker with the amount of postage printed on it to affix to the package, or run the envelope through the machine so the postage is printed directly on the envelope.

About Meters and Scales

Postage meters can come with a variety of features, but most are fairly simple, with a keypad for entering the dollar amount and a lever or button you press to print out the postage. Many print the postage directly onto the envelope you will insert into the machine. Labels are sometimes printed directly by the machine, and sometimes inserted by hand, depending on the model available. Be sure to keep the date stamp set accurately on the postage meter.

A second machine, vital to the postage meter, is a postage scale. These scales are calibrated to weigh envelopes and small packages, and then indicate either the weight and/or the postage due. Most scales give only the weight, so you must refer to a chart to determine how much postage is required, depending on which class or service you select.

Using Postage Charts

Your local post office will provide you, free of charge, with a current postage chart. If one is not displayed near your postage meter, you may wish to put one there. This chart allows you to calculate how much postage is required to send mail via the U.S. Postal Service. All you need to know is the weight of the item being sent and the type of service you want. Most business mail is sent first-class.

Keeping Copier Logs

Office photocopies can become very expensive in the overhead costs of running an office. For this reason, many businesses track the use of the photocopier in order to bill clients or charge individual departments for their usage.

If your firm does this, learn the procedures and be sure to follow them. Usually, these procedures involve keeping a log or filling out forms and indicating (normally with a numeric code) whom the copies are to be charged to.

Training Courses

Your company may offer you training as part of your job or as a benefit. Do your best to take advantage of this opportunity. By accepting training, you will develop skills important in performing your job and qualifying yourself for advancement.

Some courses typically offered to secretaries include Time Management, Computer Skills, Programming and Software, Records Management, Bookkeeping, Telephone Techniques, Dictation, Typing, Customer Service, and Meeting Management.

If your company doesn't have a training program, you may still be able to get them to pay for classes at other locations. Approach your boss if you find a class you would like to take, and present a well thought-out "sales pitch" for the course. Focus on how your boss and the company will benefit from your taking the class.

Whenever you take a course, try to apply your new skills and knowledge on the job as soon as possible. This demonstrates to your boss your ability to learn and grow, and reinforces what you have learned.

Working with a Computer Consultant

If you work with a computer, your company probably has a computer consultant. This person may be on staff or an independent contractor who is available for service, training, and programming. Introduce yourself to the consultant and cultivate a good working relationship. Many small and large problems come up with amazing regularity when you work with computers. Having access to an expert who will help you solve these problems can mean the difference between minutes and hours in finding a good solution.

Getting Service for Software, Hardware, Phone, or Fax

If you do not have a computer consultant available, you still have many options. As long as the equipment and software used in your office is registered with the manufacturer, you can call the manufacturer for service and assistance. Some expense may be involved, as the number is often long-distance (unless you happen to work in Southern California), and you may be billed for the assistance provided. Be prepared to be kept on hold while waiting for a technician to answer your call.

While such service from the manufacturer has its disadvantages, the quality of information you will receive far outweighs any inconvenience.

Another resource available to you is the sales representative who sold the equipment to your company. These people are usually aware of all the features and how to use them.

If you have service contracts on your equipment, you can place an order for a technician to come directly to your office to fix problems. This is especially important with photocopies.

The preceding advice applies to all automated office equipment, as well as the programs and software they use.

Creating Envelopes on Your PC

Many secretarial stations, instead of becoming streamlined with the installation of the computer, simply became more complex, with half a dozen pieces of equipment placed on a desk that formerly housed only a typewriter and a telephone. If you still have a typewriter being used exclusively for typing addresses on envelopes, as most secretaries do, learn how to do envelopes with your computer system and move the typewriter elsewhere. Look in your manual, call the consultant, or ask the manufacturer of your word-processing software. It may take a little time to learn how to use this function, but it is well worth the effort in terms of space.

What Else Can Your Computer Do?

When you begin your job, make time to become familiar with the way your company uses computer equipment. If you don't know the software program, contact the word-processing, computer, or training department and find out what resources are available for learning the program. Then use them. Your most important source of information will probably be fellow workers. It seems that every department or office has its own local "computer expert." This person will probably be able to help, but don't take up too much of her time, as that will prevent her from doing the job she was hired to do.

Keeping Up with New Developments

Since the computer is becoming a part of most people's work lives, it is a tool you are expected to know well. Your job performance will probably be measured in part by how well you use this piece of equipment. Keeping abreast of developments in computers can be interesting, and can help you do your job better. The easiest way to keep track of current developments is to read computer magazines and articles in the newspaper. You don't have to be an expert. By skimming these publications you can keep aware of progress and new products in just a few minutes each month.

PART FOUR

LETTER AND MEMO SKILLS

Much of your work as a secretary is preparing letters, memos, and reports. Part IV provides a broad sweep of details to help you do a more professional job in writing letters or memos and in preparing company reports.

Many sections of specific books can aid you in a particular field. If, for instance, you become a secretary in a naval office, you will need to know how to address officers of various grades and how to write a "Navy letter." The Department of the Navy has prepared correspondence handbooks with titles, addresses, and forms of address, and Navy letter characteristics. We do not provide that kind of material here: if you are not in a naval office, the information is of little use to you; if you are in a naval office, it is needless repetition.

Likewise, if you are a secretary in a Roman Catholic chancery, you need to learn all the titles and proper forms of address for several varieties of clergy (from Pope to novitiate), nuns, and brothers. These titles and forms are readily available in every chancery office; in an Episcopalian diocese's office, the titles and forms of address are noticeably different, and even more so if you work in a Baptist convention office.

The letter, memo, and report skills presented in this section are useful in any kind of corporation or institution. These suggestions are general in nature; you will have to fill in around them all the specific styles, titles, and forms used in your situation.

CHAPTER TWENTY-ONE

Grammar and Sentence Structure

For much of your transcribing work, you will have little impact on the final wording of what you type. Your boss has dictated what he wants to write, and that is that. However, depending on the way you and your boss work out the nature of your job, you may increasingly have the opportunity to write letters and reports on your own.

This book is not a detailed guide to grammar, spelling, usage, and writing. Many excellent books are available to meet those needs. You may wish to add them to your professional bookshelf for ready reference. Here, however, are some general suggestions for business writing:

1. Write in the active rather than the passive voice. Instead of saying, "It is desired that . . ." (passive voice), say, "We hope that . . ." (active voice). Rather than, "It is requested that you send . . ." (passive voice), say, "Please send . . ." (active voice). The passive voice is weak as well as impersonal. Often business and government executives have been taught to avoid intruding their own personality into business correspondence, so they use the passive voice extensively. If your boss is thoroughly conditioned in this way, he will feel comfortable only when he cannot be seen behind the flood of words it takes to phrase everything in a passive manner.

But increasingly corporate executives are urged in business schools and government workers are encouraged in style memos to express themselves actively and personally

> **Tip**
>
> Most business readers will glance at your letter in the middle of a busy day, grasp its main point if it stands out clearly, and skim over the rest.

in their correspondence. If your boss is trying to be more direct in his correspondence and has turned over to you the writing of standard routine replies, think "active" when you write your letters.

2. Make your paragraph a unit of thought. A paragraph should contain one main idea. That idea is expressed or summed up in one sentence in the paragraph. The other sentences in the paragraph help introduce the idea, give a fuller explanation, or provide reasons to support it. If you introduce a second main idea, create another paragraph for that thought.

In business correspondence, a paragraph can sometimes consist of a single sentence. Most paragraphs, however, take more than one sentence, because the writer wants to flesh out his idea more fully. Just as a business letter should normally have one subject, which can be highlighted for easy reference and filing, so each paragraph should have one idea about the subject, which can be underlined for rapid scanning.

Usually, writing is clearest if the first sentence of the paragraph contains the main idea. The reader does not have to search through the paragraph for clues about what you consider important. The point of business correspondence is to be clear, direct, uncomplicated. To hide the main idea somewhere in the middle of the paragraph complicates the process of interpreting what you mean and how committed you are to the idea.

If a paragraph builds on the idea of the previous paragraph, you help the reader make the transition by using such words or phrases as "therefore," "however," "as we said before," and so on. Think about how long a paragraph should be. Your reader will get lost in a very long paragraph, even though it has only one main idea.

Help the reader avoid the confusion of a very long paragraph by breaking it into two or three shorter paragraphs at points where the content takes a step forward in its development. Not only can a reader become lost in too long a paragraph, he can also be distracted by a series of very short paragraphs. The reader needs time—and material in the paragraph to fill in an idea with some content—to take in and think over each idea a little before having another one thrust upon him.

Remember that most business readers will glance at your letter in the middle of a busy day, grasp its main point if it stands out clearly, and skim over the rest. Your skill in crafting a letter that contains the main ideas in an obvious position and in clear language will aid them as they attempt to understand what you want to communicate.

3. Do away with needless words. Most business letters could have up to half their words taken out—and become better letters. This is especially true of dictated letters. A dictator often rambles as he tries to come up with the best way to express an idea. He

may even rephrase the idea in two or three different sentences in his search for the best way to communicate it. If he were writing the letter by hand or on a typewriter, he would probably delete the less successful attempts. But now they are on the tape, and it is too much trouble to go back over and redictate now that he has come up with the wording he wants. So the "thinking out loud" flavor remains in the letter.

If this is an important letter, you and your boss may have a standing agreement that you can type out a double-spaced draft for him to review and tighten up. This does not mean every sentence has to be short. It suggests unnecessary words should be struck out. For instance, "there is no question but that . . ." can become "without question"; "this is a matter that" becomes "this matter"; "dedicated to transportation purposes" might be "used for transportation"; "owing to the fact that" is better simply as "since"; and "call your attention to the fact that" can be "notify" or "remind you."

Positive statements are usually more concise than negative circumlocutions: "it is not without reason that" should be "it is reasonable that" or "my reason for." And, "The loss for the fourth quarter was not inconsiderable in the light of general economic trends," might be, "Our fourth-quarter loss was greater than expected, given general economic trends."

You should not make the recipient read a sentence over and over to figure out what you are trying to say, however subtly you want to phrase your point. In business correspondence, he should get your meaning clearly in one reading. Unnecessary words make it harder to unravel your meaning.

4. Keep an eye out for misplaced antecedents. An antecedent is something connected that precedes. In grammar it refers to the word, phrase, or clause to which a relative pronoun refers. A relative pronoun is the "who," "which," "it," "that," or "they" in a sentence such as "He who laughs last laughs best." "He" is the antecedent of "who" in that sentence.

It is very easy in a long, complex sentence—especially when it is being dictated—to separate the antecedent and its relative pronoun by so many ideas and words that the relative pronoun (with its accompanying clause) gets attached to the wrong antecedent. This results in confusion or ludicrous phrases. The sentence, "The captain of the ship with the two stacks that sailed illegally into New York harbor was called up to a court of inquiry," raises the image of two smokestacks sailing into the harbor. In this sentence, "ship" is the proper antecedent of "that sailed into New York harbor." But because "with the two stacks" gets placed between the rightful antecedent and its relative pronoun, the clear sense intended got muddled.

The rule of thumb is that a relative pronoun and its clause should follow immediately or as close as possible after the word it is related to. Whenever you see a relative pronoun, look back to the word it follows to

---

Tip

Positive statements are usually more concise than negative circumlocutions.

> **Tip**
>
> Trust your ear for normal, standard English. Listening to the sound and sense of the sentence will help you avoid stilted expressions.

see if the sentence makes straightforward sense. Adjust the sentence or divide it so that it makes straightforward sense. Write, "The captain of the two-stack ship that sailed illegally into New York harbor was called up to a court of inquiry." Or, "The captain of the ship that sailed illegally into New York harbor was called up to a court of inquiry. His ship was a two-stacker." Or, "The captain was called up to a court of inquiry for sailing his ship, which has two stacks, illegally into New York harbor."

Take another example. "The snow fell for two days on the house and it melted." The sun has to be especially hot to melt a house. A better way of expressing the idea would be, "After falling on the house for two days, the snow melted." The statement, "The contracts were sent to both parties, and they were not legal" contains the same kind of misplaced antecedent. The writer means to say that the contracts were not properly drawn up, not to cast aspersions on the ethics of the contracting parties. The sentence could be rewritten, "The contracts were sent in all good faith to both parties. However, careful reading showed that the documents were incorrectly drawn up." Or, "The contracts, which were not legally prepared, were sent to both parties."

5. Think more about how a sentence sounds than about following strict rules of grammar. Trust your ear for normal, standard English. Not only have you learned standard English in school, but you hear it every day on radio and television. News programs and documentaries especially use educated—but not pretentious—language in an easy, flowing manner. Your ear would be jarred if Dan Rather misused the language, for example, by saying, "they wasn't," even though you might be at a loss to describe instantly in grammatical terms what was wrong.

It is quite permissible to split an infinitive ("to carefully decide after studying all sides of the problem"), to end a sentence with a preposition ("I need some petty cash to pay the bills with"), and to use "me" instead of "I" in such phrases as, "If anyone should represent the company at the meeting, it's me." "I" may be formally correct, but "me" strikes the ear as normal.

Listening to the sound and sense of the sentence will help you to avoid stilted expressions. Equally, you will readily sense that some expressions might sound too breezy or slangy for a business letter. Such breeziness results from a desire to draw attention to yourself; it's as though you are saying, "Look at me—look how clever I am." And when you do that, the reader is so distracted by his opinion of your attempted cleverness that he may never focus on the point of the correspondence.

CHAPTER TWENTY-TWO

Spelling

It is well-known that English is a very difficult language to spell. It is not consistently phonetic; that is, every written consonant and vowel does not always represent the same sound. *G* is sometimes a hard sound, as in "gruff"; it is sometimes a soft sound, as in "gem"; it is sometimes used with other consonants to represent an "*f*-type" sound, as in "enough"; and sometimes it is in the spelling, but represents no sound at all, as in "bough."

English has developed from many languages, borrowing words and phrases from all. Rooted in early Anglo-Saxon, mixed with Celtic and Latin, then Norman, and borrowing heavily from Greek, French, German, Norse, and Arabic, this complex language has been richly seasoned by Spanish, Chinese, Japanese, American Indian, and numerous African languages. In each case, words that have entered arrived with their original spelling and pronunciation. In time the pronunciation changed to be more in conformity with developing tones of English, whereas the spelling tended to remain in the native form. This has created all kinds of so-called inconsistencies in our language that purists from time to time try, without success, to correct. We are slow (not "slo") to accept linguistic changes, though we are quick to invent informal language and borrow elements from other languages when it is useful to do so.

Many English spellings reflect the sounds that were once part of the word when it was first used in the language: in "night" the *gh*

> **Tip**
> English has developed from many languages, borrowing words and phrases from all.

was once pronounced as a kind of guttural consonant in the back of the throat, similar to such sounds in German today. That consonant was lost in English, but the spelling lingers on. "Nite" is still ad-speak, not accepted English. The same is true of "high"; but we still accept "hiway" only in traffic signs, where the need is to use as few letters as possible. This is also true of "through" and "thruway."

Other English spellings reflect the standard in the language from which they were borrowed: "petit" is from French and means "small" or "tiny" or "minor." But in English, it is pronounced the same as "petty," which generally means "trivial," "trifling," or "insignificant." Thus, we have "petit juries," as compared with "grand juries"; "petit point" (involving intricate, detailed needlework); and "petit fours" (small, rich tea cakes). You need to know the difference between "petit" and "petty" to use the correct spelling. Indeed, some juries can be petty, as well as petit.

Plurals often present a spelling problem, since the plural form is usually related to the language from which the word was borrowed. In some words, the plural is the same as the singular: "marquis" is both singular and plural, although some English writers have given the English-style plural to the word in the form of "marquises." So now both "marquis" and "marquises" are correct English plurals for the singular "marquis." In other words, the plural form in English is often based on the original language in its construction: "index" is

"indices," according to the Latin original. And many writers still use this form. However, many are using the English-style form of "indexes."

In certain words borrowed from Greek, the singular ends in *um* and the plural in *a*. A "phylum" is a major division of the animal kingdom. Several such divisions are "phyla." However, this is not a hard-and-fast rule. A scientific word borrowed from Greek is "pseudopodium," meaning "false foot." It refers to certain one-celled animals, such as an amoeba, which advance a part of their protoplasm to encircle and absorb a speck of food or to move from one place to another (the animal flows into the part it sent out, drawing the rest of itself into the new location, and then sends out a new pseudopodium to continue its movement). More than one of these "false feet" are "pseudopodia." So far, this follows the "phylum-phyla" pattern for Greek words; however, the singular of "pseudopodia" now often is "pseudopod," and the plural of "pseudopod" increasingly is seen in the work of some writers as "pseudopods."

For purists, the singular for "media" is "medium." Thus, TV is a "medium," but TV and newspapers are "media." However, in popular usage "medium" sounds stilted in many sentences where it is really proper: "Could anyone ever replace Walter Cronkite as a *medium* personality?" The singular of "data" is "datum." Most people outside the scientific community now use "data" as both the singular and plural form.

Accurate spelling is a result of early drill

work in school. Also, the more you know of other languages, the more you will understand spelling patterns and variances. Accurate spelling can be achieved and developed by frequent use of a dictionary and a speller wordbook. A speller wordbook (usually called a "speller-divider" since it also includes word-division breaks) is a simple alphabetical listing—without definition—of thousands of words. A good speller book will have about 50,000 words. It shows not only the spelling of the main word, but also derivatives and alternate spellings:

me-chan-ic
me-chan-i-cal
me-chan-i-cal-ly
me-chan-ics
mech-a-nism
mech-a-nis-tic
mech-a-nis-ti-cal-ly
mech-a-ni-za-tion
mech-a-nize
mech-a-nized
mech-a-niz-ing

Or:
fo-cal
fo-cal-ly
fo-cus
pl., fo-cus-es or fo-ci
v., fo-cused or fo-cussed
   fo-cus-ing or fo-cus-sing

These books give no definitions, but show complete spelling patterns for every generally used word in English.

If your work calls for extensive legal language, get a speller for legal terms; the same applies for medical terms. These wordbooks or spellers are available from any well-stocked reference section in a bookstore or office-supply store. Whenever you have any doubt about how to spell a word, look it up in your speller. You will find the speller much easier and faster to use than a dictionary. The dictionary is essential when you need to know the meaning of a word, or have to decide which word to use where alternatives can be easily confused. If you are uncertain whether to use "proceed" or "precede," go to your dictionary to determine which is the proper word for the context in which you are using it. The speller will not help you resolve that question. However, if you know the proper word is "proceed," the speller will remind you not to misspell it "procede."

It is helpful to be aware of some problem spelling areas. If you are prone to make mistakes in any of the areas, take extra care to use your speller when you encounter a word in one of your problem zones. In time, you will find that particular word no longer a problem, but if you do not use it for a long time, it may be a problem again when you meet it.

Problem spelling areas include:

1. Words that end in -*ence* or -*ance*, -*ent* or -*ant*. Keep using your speller. Even when you feel positive about a spelling, you can be mistaken.

2. When to make a plural by adding -*s* or -*es*. If the word is only one syllable and the addition of the plural will still keep it one syllable, -*s* is usually added: kite/kites, girl/girls, scene/scenes, light/lights, toy/toys.

If another syllable is added when making the plural, -*es* is usually added: glass/glasses, wish/wishes, wrench/wrenches. If the word ends with *o* and that *o* follows a vowel, the plural is generally made by adding

-s: rodeo/rodeos, patio/patios, radio/radios, ratio/ratios, taboo/taboos.

If, however, the word ends with *o* and that *o* follows a consonant, the plural is generally made by adding *-es:* tomato/tomatoes, zero/zeroes, echo/echoes, potato/potatoes. (The general rule has some exceptions—especially for musical terms, as in alto/altos or piano/pianos—so use your speller when in doubt.)

3. When to use *ie* or *ei*. The old school verse generally can be followed: use *i* before *e* except after *c*, or when the word has a sound like *ay*, as in *weigh*. This verse applies when the *ie* or *ei* combination is sounded as a single vowel, but not when it is two distinct vowels: deist, reintroduce.

4. When to double a final consonant. If the word is a single syllable and ends with a single final consonant, double it when adding a suffix that is also a single syllable and begins with a vowel (*-ed, -er, -ing*): trip/tripping, big/bigger, stop/stopped.

If the word ends in a single final consonant and has two or more syllables, with the accent on the last syllable, double the final consonant when adding the one-syllable suffix that begins with a vowel: begin/beginning, refer/referred, occur/occurrence, omit/omitted.

If a word has two vowels in front of the final single consonant, do not double the consonant when adding the suffix: read/reader, keep/keeper (thus bookkeeping), feel/feeling, boil/boiling. If a word normally ends in two consonants, do not double the last one when adding the suffix: damp/damper, pick/picking, gulp/gulping, help/helping.

If a word ends in a single final consonant and the last syllable of the word is not stressed (the accent is earlier in the word), do not double the final consonant when adding the suffix: profit/profited, jewel/jeweler, benefit/benefiting.

If the word ends in a single consonant with the accent on the last syllable, and that accent shifts forward when the suffix is added, do not double the final consonant for that suffix (but do double it if the accent remains in the same place when the suffix is added): refer/reference, but referred; confer/conference, but conferring; prefer/preference, but preferred.

If a word ends in *x*, do not double the *x* when adding a suffix: box/boxing, mix/mixed, fix/fixer. When in doubt, use your dictionary to look up the word and the form it takes when a suffix is added. A speller is less likely to contain these forms of the word.

5. Whether to keep the final *e* when adding a suffix. Generally, keep the *e* in words that end with a silent *e* when adding a suffix that begins with a consonant, but drop the *e* when adding a suffix that begins with a vowel: force/forceful/forcing, love/lovely/lovable, use/useless/usage. In American English, this rule is usually not followed when *-ment* is added: judge/judgment, acknowledge/acknowledgment.

If the word ends in *ce* or *ge*, keep the *e*

Tip

Accurate spelling is a matter of early drill work in school. The more you know of other languages, the more you will understand spelling patterns and variances.

Tip

When in doubt, look up the word in your dictionary.

---

when the suffix begins with an *a* or *o* (to keep the sound "soft"): notice/noticeable, but noticing; manage/manageable, but managing; service/serviceable, but servicing; and courage/courageous.

In verbs, a final *ie* is changed to *y* before adding *-ing:* die/dying, lie/lying, tie/tying. A final *oe* is unchanged when adding *-ing:* canoe/canoeing, hoe/hoeing, shoe/shoeing. For each of these general rules, it is always possible to encounter an exception. Keep your speller handy. Your confidence about sensing the right spelling of a word will develop as you continue to use your speller and dictionary.

If you use a word processor with a spell-check function, use the spell-check at the conclusion of each job and after you finish revising a job. This dictionary will catch obvious typos and force you to double-check complex words. It will not alert you to words that are spelled correctly but used wrongly: *fiend* for *friend, follow* for *following, contexts* for *contents*. To catch misspellings of this nature, you have to proofread the job both for spelling and for sense.

Poor spelling reflects badly on your boss. People who receive a letter from her with a misspelling will think less highly of her. It also reflects badly on you. Your boss might manifest her anger for your making her look foolish or ignorant, or she might try to be nice about it, hiding her anger. An occasional blooper can be forgiven, but a continued pattern of poor spelling may soon result in your transfer or worse. Your boss would much rather wait a few minutes for you to check any doubtful spelling so you can present her with work you can both take professional pride in.

CHAPTER TWENTY-THREE

Word Division

Normally word division is not a factor in most of your business correspondence. You type letters, memos, and reports flush left, ragged right. Whole words end a line and whole words begin the next line. By not dividing words at the end of a line, you save yourself a great deal of time. You also save yourself the possibility of making errors by dividing the word at the wrong place.

Word division becomes a factor when you have a big gap at the end of a line because the last word of that line is long and would go too far over the margin to look presentable. Rather than leave the gap, you decide to divide the word. In routine business correspondence, this may happen only ten or twenty times a week.

Word division becomes a major factor if you use a word processor for long reports and your boss wants the report justified (flush left and flush right). In order to fill in space for justified printing, you need to divide many words—three or four in a single paragraph.

Keep in mind the basic rule for word division. In America, words are divided according to pronunciation. This can result in strange-looking divisions, unless you understand this rule. For instance, "knowl-edge" is divided into two syllables: *knowl* and *edge*. You may think the word should be divided as "know-ledge," until you consider how you pronounce the word.

The rule will sometimes change the place a word is divided as the accent shifts from one syllable to another when you add prefixes or suffixes. Take, for instance, the word "refer." The word is divided "re-fer," with the accent on *fer*. However, when you add the suffix *-ence*, the accent shifts to the first syllable, and the sounds making up that first syllable change: "ref-er-ence." And if you add the suffix *-ing*, the accent stays on *-fer*: "re-fer-ring."

A number of speller-divider books are published by companies that also publish dictionaries. Most of these contain about 50,000 general words. Specialized speller-divider books are available for legal and medical words. If, for instance, you work in a law office, a legal speller-divider is essential.

In Chapter 22 (Spelling), we indicated how these books should be used to insure your spelling is as accurate as possible. When dividing words, use the book to double-check any division you have a doubt about. In the book publishing business, one of the most common reasons for sending a set of proofs back to the printer for reworking is improper word division. Today's electronic text management systems, whether photocomposition or your word-processing system, have hyphenation programs. If these programs are used on an automatic setting to divide words according to a program's logic, many errors will occur. The computer does not pronounce words and therefore does not know when a syllable shifts in human pronunciation. The computer follows a straightforward set of logical rules that is right about 85 percent of the time. It is that 15 percent of word divisions that you have to insure are correct.

The accent on some words shifts when the word is used as a verb instead of a noun. And with the shift of accent, a shift in word division occurs: "Des-ert"—with the accent on the first syllable—is a noun, meaning "a barren region," but "de-sert"—with the accent on the last syllable—is a verb, meaning "to abandon." "Pres-ent"—with the accent on the first syllable—is a noun, meaning "a gift"; "pre-sent"—with the accent on the last syllable—is a verb, meaning "to offer or give." English is replete with examples of similar noun/verb words in which the spelling is the same but the pronunciation is different.

The pattern of changing accents happens among variations of a word. For instance, "pre-sen-ta-tion" has a different accent from "pre-sent-able." The shift of accent changes the location of the division of the word. As in spelling, several rules will guide you correctly most of the time. And as in spelling, when in doubt, look it up. Several basic word-division rules follow:

1. A single-syllable word is not divided: "boy," "car," "time." This is true even if a suffix is added to the word, but the pronunciation continues to be a single syllable: "maimed," "rhymed," "helped," "gasped," "spelled," "mired."

2. Suffixes that are generally pronounced as a single syllable are not divided further: -ceous, -cial, -cion, -cious, -geous, -gion, -gious, -sial, -sion, -tion, and -tial. Thus, "region" is divided into "re-gion," not "re-gi-on"; "courageous" is "cou-ra-geous," not "cou-rage-ous."

3. A final syllable in which the only sound is an *l* or *bull* should not be divided from the preceding syllable: "pre-sent-able," not "pre-sent-a-ble"; "pos-sible," not "possi-ble"; "title," not "ti-tle"; "read-able," not "read-a-ble"; "people," not "peo-ple."

4. Where possible, when a vowel alone forms a syllable, make the division after the vowel: "criti-cal," not "crit-ical"; "habi-tat," not "hab-itat."

5. If pronunciation permits, word division can normally take place between two consonants when they are located between two vowels: "foun-da-tion," not "found-a-tion";

Tip

Keep in mind a basic rule for word division. In America, words are divided according to pronunciation.

Tip

Whenever possible, personal names should not be divided. When it is necessary, the name should be broken after the middle initial.

"moun-tain," not "mount-ain"; "par-tisan," not "part-i-san."

6. Division between syllables should not be made where one syllable has only one letter. In the samples that follow, the entire word should be on one line: "able," "again," "among," "abort," "enough," "even," "item," "unite," "unit."

7. Dividing a word in which one syllable has two letters is acceptable at the end of a line, but should be avoided, if possible, at the beginning of a line: "un-sung," "il-lusion," "em-bassy," "am-nesia," but not "loss-es," "mon-ey," "flat-ly," "liv-en."

8. Where possible, when compound words are divided, they should be divided at the hyphen: "decision-making," not "deci-sion-making."

9. Words that were once compound words but have now become so standard that they are considered to be single words should be divided, as much as possible, at their natural breaks: "rough-housing," rather than "roughhous-ing"; "weather-man," rather than "weath-erman"; "harbor-master," rather than "harbormas-ter."

10. If a word has a prefix, division after the prefix is better than elsewhere in the word: "pseudo-podia," rather than "pseudopo-dia" or "pseu-dopodia"; "dis-il-lusion," rather than "disil-lusion"; "non-sectarian," rather than "nonsec-tarian"; "un-savory," rather than "unsa-vory."

Telephone numbers should never be divided. If the area code is in parentheses, it is possible—not preferable—to end a line with the area code and begin the next line with the telephone number.

Whenever possible, personal names should not be divided. When it is necessary, the name should be broken after the middle initial. If the name consists of the first and second initials followed by the last name, the break should be only after the second initial. Thus,

Best: Jonathan R. Buckingham
First choice, if a break is needed: Jonathan R. (break) Buckingham
Second choice, if a break is needed: Jonathan R. Buck-ingham
Third choice: Jonathan R. Bucking-ham
Fourth choice: Jona-than R. Buckingham

Best: T. S. Eliot
Permissible, if a break is needed: T. S. (break) Eliot
Not permissible: T. (break) S. Eliot

If abbreviations are used with figures, the figures and the abbreviations should never be separated on two different lines: 8:15 A.M.; 450 cm; 210 mi.; 25 gal.

Divide words as seldom as possible, but when you have a job in which you have to divide them throughout the project, glance through these suggestions before you begin to refresh your memory on the basic principles. Then use your speller-divider throughout the task whenever you have a question.

CHAPTER TWENTY-FOUR

Compound Words

Compound Words

Compound words are a secretary's nightmare. When are they used as two separate words? When are they joined by a hyphen? When do they become so well established that they are joined into a new single word?

The most complete and easiest-to-understand summary of good usage for compound words is contained in a table in *A Manual of Style*, published by The University of Chicago press. Rather than try to summarize all the information in the table, it is clearer just to reprint the table here for your ready reference:

A Spelling Guide for Compound Words

TYPE COMPOUND	SIMILAR COMPOUNDS	REMARKS
Noun Forms		
master builder	master artist, master wheel *but:* mastermind, masterpiece, mastersinger, masterstroke	Spell temporary compounds with *master* open.
fellow employee	brother officer, mother church, father figure, foster child, parent organization	*Type:* word of relationship + noun. Spell all such compounds open.
decision making	problem solving, coal mining, bird watching	*Type:* object + gerund. Spell temporary compounds open. Many closed permanent compounds (e.g., *bookkeeping, dressmaking*) will be found in the dictionary. See also under Adjective Forms, below.
quasi corporation	quasi contract, quasi scholar, quasi union	Spell *quasi* noun compounds open. But see under Adjective Forms, below.

TYPE COMPOUND	SIMILAR COMPOUNDS	REMARKS
	Noun Forms—Continued	
attorney general	postmaster general, surgeon general, judge advocate general	Safe to spell all similar compounds open.
vice-president	vice-chancellor, vice-consul *but:* viceroy, vicegerent, vice admiral	Temporary compounds with *vice-* are best hyphenated: *vice-manager, vice-chief.*
scholar-poet	author-critic, city-state, soldier-statesman	*Type:* noun + noun, representing different and equally important functions. Hyphenate.
grandfather	grandniece, grandnephew	Close up all *grand-* relatives.
brother-in-law	mother-in-law, sisters-in-law	Hyphenate all *in-laws.*
great-grandson	great-great-grandmother	Hyphenate all *great-* relatives.
self-restraint	self-knowledge, self-consciousness	Hyphenate all *self-* compounds. See also under Adjective Forms, below.
Johnny-on-the spot	light-o'-love, Alice-sit-by-the fire, stay-at-home, stick-in-the mud *but:* flash in the pan, ball of fire	*Type:* combination of words including a prepositional phrase describing a character. Hyphenate any new creations.
one-half	two-thirds, four and five-sevenths *but:* thirty-one hundredths, three sixty-fourths	*Type:* spelled-out fractional number. Connect numerator and denominator with a hyphen unless either already contains a hyphen.
president-elect	senator-elect, mayor-elect *but:* county assessor elect	Hyphenate *-elect* compounds unless the name of the office is in two or more words.
headache	toothache, stomachache	Spell compounds with *-ache* solid.

TYPE COMPOUND	SIMILAR COMPOUNDS	REMARKS
	Noun Forms—*Continued*	
checkbook	notebook, textbook, pocketbook, storybook *but:* reference book	Permanent compounds with *-book* are solid except for a few unwieldy ones. Temporary compounds should be spelled open: *pattern book, recipe book.*
boardinghouse	boathouse, clubhouse, greenhouse, clearinghouse *but:* rest house, business house	Permanent compounds with *-house* are solid; temporary ones, mainly open.
ex-president	ex-husband, ex-mayor, ex–corporate executive	Compounds with *ex-* meaning *former* are hyphenated (en dash when the second part is an open compound). Seldom used in formal writing, where *former* is preferred.
	Adjective Forms	
highly developed species	poorly seen, barely living, wholly invented, highly complex	*Type:* adverb ending in *-ly* + participle or adjective. Always open.
long-lived	much-loved, ever-fruitful, still-active	*Type:* adverb other than the *-ly* type + participle or adjective. Now usually hyphenated before the noun.
Central European countries	Old English, Scotch Presbyterian, New Testament, Civil War, Latin American	*Type:* compound formed from unhyphenated proper names. Always open. (Do not confuse with such forms as *Scotch-Irish, Austro-Hungarian.*)
sodium chloride solution	sulfuric acid, calcium carbonate	*Type:* chemical terms. Leave open.

TYPE COMPOUND	SIMILAR COMPOUNDS	REMARKS
	Adjective Forms—*Continued*	
grand prix racing	a priori, post mortem, Sturm und Drang *but:* laissez-faire	*Type:* foreign phrase used as an adjective. Leave open unless hyphenated in original language.
bluish green paint	gray blue, emerald green, coal black, reddish orange	*Type:* color term in which first element modifies the second. Leave open.
blue-green algae	red-green color blindness, black-and-white print	*Type:* color term in which elements are of equal importance. Hyphenate.
self-reliant boy	self-sustaining, self-righteous, self-confident, self-effacing *but:* selfless, selfsame, unselfconscious	Hyphenate *self-* compounds whether they precede or follow the noun. See also under Noun Forms, above.
decision-making procedures	curiosity-evoking dust-catching, thirst-quenching, dissension-producing, interest-bearing	*Type:* object + present participle. Hyphenate all before the noun and a few permanent compounds (e.g., *thought-provoking*) after the noun.
twenty-odd performances	sixty-odd, fifteen-hundred-odd, 360-odd	*Type:* cardinal number + *odd*. Hyphenate before or after the noun.
ten-foot pole	three-mile limit, 100-yard dash, one-inch margin, 10-meter band, four-year-old boy *but:* 10 percent increase	*Type:* cardinal number + unit of measurement. Hyphenate compound if it precedes noun.
well-known man	ill-favored girl, well-intentioned person *but:* very well known man; he is well known	Compounds with *well-, ill-, better-, best-, little-, lesser-,* etc., are hyphenated before the noun unless expression carries a modifier.

TYPE COMPOUND	SIMILAR COMPOUNDS	REMARKS
	Adjective Forms—*Continued*	
high-, low-level job	high-class, high-energy, low-test, low-lying *but:* highborn, highbrow, lowbred	With few exceptions, *high-* and *low-* adjectival compounds are hyphenated in any position.
matter-of-fact approach	devil-may-care attitude, a how-to book, everything is up-to-date	*Type:* phrase used as adjective. Hyphenate in any position.
quasi-public corporation	quasi-judicial, quasi-legislative, quasi-stellar	Hyphenate adjectival *quasi-* compounds whether they precede or follow the noun. But see under Noun Forms, above.
half-baked plan	half-asleep, half-blooded, half-cocked, half-timbered *but:* halfhearted, halfway	Hyphenate adjectival *half-* compounds whether they precede or follow the noun.
two-thirds majority	The project is three-fourths completed. He was one-fourth white.	Common fractions used as adjectives or adverbs are hyphenated.
cross-town expressway	cross-country, cross-fertile, cross-grained *but:* crossbred, crosscut, crosshatched, crosswise	Any temporary adjectival *cross-* compounds can be safely hyphenated.
all-inclusive study	all-around, all-powerful, all-out	Hyphenate *all-* compounds whether they precede or follow the noun.
coarse-grained wood	able-bodied, pink-faced, straight-sided, even-handed	*Type:* adjective + past participle derived from a noun. Hyphenate such compounds when they precede the noun. After the noun they can generally be left open.

TYPE COMPOUND	SIMILAR COMPOUNDS	REMARKS
	Adjective Forms—*Continued*	
catlike movements	fencelike, gridlike, saillike (*or* sail-like), basilicalike (*or* basilica-like) *always:* Tokyo-like, gull-like, vacuum-bottle-like	The suffix *-like* is freely used to form new compounds, which are generally spelled solid except for those formed from proper names, words ending in *ll*, and word combinations. Some also prefer to hyphenate when the base word ends in a single *l* or consists of three or more syllables.
a **tenfold** increase	twofold, multifold *but:* 25-fold	Adjectival compounds with *-fold* are spelled solid unless they are formed with figures.
a **statewide** referendum	worldwide, boroughwide, parishwide, archdiocese wide (*or* archdiocese-wide)	*Type:* word denoting a geographical, political, or social division + *-wide.* Close up unless the compound is long and cumbersome.

Words with Prefixes

A few words that might be considered word-forming prefixes appear in the columns of the table on pages 148–152, and most of the adjectival forms are hyphenated. The word-forming prefixes in the table on page 154 (the list is not exhaustive) form compounds that are nearly always closed, whether they are nouns, verbs, adjectives, or adverbs. Here are the chief exceptions to the closed-style rule:

1. Compounds in which the second element is a capitalized word or a numeral: anti-Semitic, un-American, pre-1914, post-Kantian, Anti-Federalist. Compounds that must be distinguished from homonyms: re-cover, un-ionized, sometimes re-create.

2. Compounds in which the second element consists of more than one word: pre-latency-period therapy, non-English-speaking people, pre–Civil War. (In the last, note the en dash, used before an open compound.)

3. A few compounds in which the last letter of the prefix is the same as the first letter of the word following.

Newly invented compounds of the last type tend to be hyphenated when they first appear in the language and become closed up when they grow more familiar. Coinages like *infra-area* and *meta-analysis*, for example, are sometimes closed up, and *intra-cellular* is now the standard form (for *meta-analysis*, however, a better choice would be *metanalysis*, since the combining prefix also exists in the form *met-*.) In addition to familiarity, appearance influences the retention of hyphens. It is never wrong to keep a hyphen in order to avoid misleading or puzzling forms: non-native, anti-intellectual.

Note also that when a prefix stands alone, it carries a hyphen: over- and underused, macro- and microeconomics.

Prefix	Examples
ante-	anteroom, antediluvian, antenatal
anti-	anticlerical, antihero, antihypertensive, *but* anti-inflammatory, anti-utopian
bi-	bivalent, biconvex, binomial
bio-	bioecology, biophysical
co-	coauthor, coordinate, coeditor, *but* co-edition, co-opt, co-op, co-worker
counter-	counterclockwise, countermeasures, countercurrent, counterblow
extra-	extraterrestrial, extrafine
infra-	infrasonic, infrastructure
inter-	interrelated, intertidal, interregnum
intra-	intraarterial, intrazonal, intracranial
macro-	macroeconomics, macrosphere, macromolecular
meta-	metalanguage, metagalaxy, metaethical, metastable
micro-	microminiaturized, microimage, micromethod
mid-	midtown, midgut
mini-	minibus, miniskirt, minibike
non-	nonviolent, nonperson, nonplus, nonnative (or non-native)
over-	overlong, overeager, overanalyzed
post- ("after")	postdoctoral, postface, postwar, postparturition
pre-	preempt, precognition, preconference, premalignant
pro-	progovernment, procathedral, procephalic
pseudo-	pseudopregnancy, pseudoclassic, pseudoheroic
re-	reedit, reunify, redigitalize, reexamine
semi-	semiopaque, semiconductor, *but* semi-independent, semi-indirect
sub-	subjacent, subbasement, subcrustal
super-	supertanker, superhigh (frequency), superpose
supra-	supranational, suprarenal, supraliminal
trans-	transoceanic, transmembrane, transsocietal
ultra-	ultrafiche, ultramontane, ultraorganized
un-	unfunded, unchurched, uncoiffed, unneutered
under-	underused, undersea, underpowered, underreport

CHAPTER TWENTY-FIVE

Abbreviations

Every professional and business specialty develops its own set of abbreviations. Whether law or medicine, chemistry or architecture, shoes or space vehicles, each specialty has a unique technical vocabulary. Often used terms within that special vocabulary get shortened or abbreviated.

If you are new to the vocabulary, the abbreviations can seem threatening. You do not know what they mean, how or when to use them, or even whether you are using the right one in the right place. But, as with any specialized vocabulary, you will soon feel quite at home with the abbreviations as well as with the words they represent. Only a limited number of these terms exist, and they usually appear over and over again.

Make up a list of abbreviations used regularly in your boss's correspondence. After the first dozen or two entries, the addition of new entries will occur only rarely. Look up each one in a dictionary (if they do not appear in the list that follows). If you cannot find a term in the dictionary, ask your boss what it means and when it is used.

Latin Abbreviations

Many abbreviations originated in Latin. If the Latin abbreviation is still used, it is most often in standard Roman typeface, rather than in italics or underlined. This is true, for instance, of *etc.* and *et al.*, as well as *vide*, *N.B.*, *i.e.*, and *e.g.*

The abbreviations and their meanings are: *etc.* from *et cetera*, meaning "and the rest" or "and so forth"; *et al.* from *et alii,* meaning "and others" (people, not things); *vid.* from *vide,* meaning "see" (a reference to a similar statement elsewhere); *N.B.* from *note bene,* meaning "note well" or "pay particular attention"; *i.e.* from *id est,* meaning "that is"; and *e.g.* from *exempli gratia,* meaning "for example" or "for instance."

However, modern American usage is moving away from Latin abbreviations. English words now take their places: *and so on* or *and so forth; and others; see; note; that is* or *I mean; for example, for instance,* or *here are some examples.* The average business reader will readily understand the English expression, but may miss the precise meaning of the Latin abbreviation. Using the English form allows greater clarity in business correspondence and avoids literary pretentiousness.

The only universally known Latin abbreviation may be *etc.* Overuse of *etc.* indicates a lack of thinking through of all the facets of a subject and hiding that lack of precision behind a familiar abbreviation.

Company Names and Organizations

You will probably use more abbreviations in names of companies and organizations than in any other circumstance. It is important to develop a consistent style for these abbreviations. Then you do not have to think about how to abbreviate each time you need to use one.

Company names often include one or more of the following as part of the formal company name: Bro., Bros., Co., Corp., Inc., Ltd., or &. In Spanish or French companies, *S.A., Inc.,* and *Ltd.* usually follow a comma. However, many corporations no longer use a comma to separate *Inc.* from the rest of the name. Look at the company's letterhead or listing in a business or trade directory to see what that particular company prefers.

The full title, including *Inc., Ltd.,* or *Corp.,* is used on envelopes and in the address section of a letter. In the body of the letter, however, *Inc.* or *Ltd.* is usually dropped when referring to the company.

Many companies abbreviate their names to initials, which often become more well-known than the full name of the company: Radio Corporation of America/RCA; International Business Machines Corporation/IBM; National Cash Register Corporation/NCR; Trans World Airlines/TWA. These abbreviations can be used without further defining them. They are normally seen without periods: TWA, not T.W.A. The same is true of government agencies, associations, unions, and other groups. Some are so well-known that the abbreviation alone is enough; however, others should be used only after the full name of the organization has been written out in full. Thus, *TVA, YMCA, NBC, AT&T, OPEC,* and *NATO* can probably be used without first writing

---

Tip

Overuse of *etc.* indicates a lack of thinking through of all the facets of a subject and hiding that lack of precision behind a catchall abbreviation.

out the name of the organization (Tennessee Valley Authority, Young Men's Christian Association, National Broadcasting Company, American Telephone & Telegraph Company, Organization of Petroleum Exporting Countries, and North Atlantic Treaty Organization). However, if your letter refers to *ASEA*, *NCRWS*, or *ABC*, you should write out the full name of the organization, follow it with the abbreviation in parentheses, and then use the abbreviation throughout the rest of the letter: American Solar Energy Association (ASEA); National Campaign for Radioactive Waste Safety (NCRWS); and American Beagle Club (ABC). With *ABC*, it is especially important to define the abbreviation by giving the full name of the organization since most readers would automatically link *ABC* to American Broadcasting Company.

Government agencies are initial-prone. If your work includes constant reference to or interaction with a number of government agencies, keep a list of the agencies and their abbreviations. The Government Printing Office (GPO) publishes an annual directory of all agencies, their abbreviations, addresses, and chief personnel with their titles.

Titles and Forms of Address

You will continually use abbreviations for titles and forms of address of people to or about whom you write. In using a title before a name, spell it out fully when the person's last name is used alone: General Eisenhower, Lieutenant Commander Jones, Congressman Udall, Senator Helms. If the person's first name, last name, and middle initial are used, the title is normally abbreviated: Gen. Dwight D. Eisenhower, Lt.

Cdr. John Q. Jones, Rep. Morris Udall, Sen. Jesse Helms. Only if you were in a naval office would you abbreviate *Lieutenant Commander* to *LCDR:* most civilians would not understand such an in-group abbreviation.

Some forms of address are always abbreviated, whether the full name or only the last name is used: Mr., Mrs., Miss, Ms., M., MM., Mme., Mlle., Dr., Sr., Sra., Srta. If the title includes a reference to *Reverend* or *Honorable*, the word is spelled out in full if it follows *the:* the Honorable Frank M. Wright; the Reverend Robert C. Parkinson; the Reverend Dr. Hightower; the Very (Most) (Right) Reverend Thomas P. Smith. But in many other cases, the title is abbreviated when used with the full name: Hon. Frank M. Wright; Rev. Robert C. Parkinson; Rt. Rev. Thomas P. Smith; Rev. Dr. Richard S. Hightower. The abbreviation is not used with just the last name: Dear Mr. Wright, not Dear Hon. Wright; Dear Bishop Smith, not Dear Rt. Rev. Smith; Dear Dr. Hightower, not Dear Rev. Dr. Hightower; Dear Mr. Parkinson, not Dear Rev. Parkinson. If Mr. Parkinson is a Roman Catholic or Episcopalian priest, it is permissible to write *Dear Father Parkinson* or *Dear Fr. Parkinson.*

Titles or degrees, when used after a name, follow a comma: John M. Packard, Sr.; John M. Packard, Jr.; Mrs. John M. Packard, Sr.; Richard B. Thorne, M.D.; the Rev. Thomas P. Ambleer, D.D.; William R. Orcutt, Esq. The only exception to this is when *I, II, or III* is a part of the name: John M. Packard III. These abbreviations are never used with just the last name: *Mr. Packard, Jr.,* is not correct.

Esq. (for Esquire) is often used in America to denote a lawyer. It is used only with the first name, middle initial, and last name;

never with *Mr.* or *Ms.* Thus, *Ellen S. Porter, Esq.*, is correct; *Ms. Ellen S. Porter, Esq.*, is not. She would be addressed as *Dear Ms. Porter.* The *Dr.* in front of a name is dropped if the degree follows the name: Richard B. Thorne, M.D., not Dr. Richard B. Thorne, M.D.

If you use a company or organizational title on the envelope or as part of the address section of the letter, the person's title follows the full name and is separated by a comma. The social form of address (Mr., Ms., Dr.) is not used when a title follows the name: Robert S. Rodney, President, not Mr. Robert S. Rodney, President; Mary K. Winters, Comptroller, not Ms. Mary K. Winters, Comptroller.

In most businesses, *Dr.* is not used as the normal way of addressing executives, even though they may have earned degrees or honorary degrees. *Dr.* is always used with medical and dental personnel; it is usually used by religious personnel, even though it may be an honorary doctorate. It is usually used in academic circles only if it is an earned doctorate.

Metric Abbreviations

Metric measurements are used in scientific writing. Increasingly, they are replacing the former English measurements; you now buy wine by the liter instead of the quart or gallon. Metric abbreviations are not followed by a period: meter/m; gram/gm; centimeter/cm; cubic centimeter/cc.

English Abbreviations

Traditional English abbreviations, however, are followed by a period: inch/in.; foot/ft.; mile/mi.; gallon/gal.; cubic yard/cu. yd.; ounce/oz.

Geography and Locations

The custom now is to use the Postal Service abbreviations for states rather than the older conventions: CA, not Calif. or Cal.; CO, not Colo.; MA, not Mass. When standing alone in the body of a letter or report (not combined with the name of a city), spell out the name of the state in full.

City names are generally not abbreviated in letters: Fort Wayne, not Ft. Wayne. The most noticeable exception to this is a city that includes the word Saint: St. Paul, St. Louis. However, spelling out the word *Saint* is entirely acceptable.

Normally, the names of countries are spelled out in full, although the United Soviet Socialist Republic (Russia) is often abbreviated to USSR. In letters, the names of streets in addresses are usually spelled out: Avenue, Drive, Lane, Street, Boulevard, Place, Road. If the address includes a quadrant of the city (NE, SW, NW, SE), that designation usually follows the street and is abbreviated: 1505 K Street, SE; *but* 837 Central Park West. *N., E., S.,* or *W.* go before a street address and usually take a period: 83 N. Elm Street.

Time

Months are usually spelled out in full, as are the days of the week. In typing, the time of day is usually in lowercase (small letters) and not underlined: 8:15 a.m., 5:45 p.m. These are abbreviations borrowed from Latin: *a.m.* (ante meridiem) means "before noon"; *p.m.* (post meridiem) means "after noon." Usually, if periods are used in an abbreviation, leave no spaces after those periods within the abbreviation itself: a.m., not a. m.; Ph.D., not Ph. D.; U.S., not U. S.; i.e., not i. e. However, use a space between the initials of a person's name: T. S. Eliot, not T.S. Eliot.

Some of the common abbreviations found in tables are not normally used in the body of a letter or report. Thus, in the report you would spell out the months, but a table within the report might use the following abbreviations to save space, especially at the heads of columns: Ja, F, Mr, Ap, My, Je, Jl, Ag, S, O, N, D, or the more familiar Jan, Feb, Mar, Apr, May, June, July, Aug, Sept, Oct, Nov, Dec. Much depends on the amount of space you have available.

CHAPTER TWENTY-SIX

Postal Service* Forms

Although you may use alternative methods of sending correspondence and small packages—ranging from air-express services to internal electronic mail—you will use the United States Postal Service (USPS) as the standard means of sending mail. The basic reasons are cost and convenience. The cost of sending a nonpriority letter is much less when it is sent through the Postal Service than when it is sent by air express. At the time of writing, it was 5,500 percent less! A letter can be dropped in a handy mail chute near the elevator on your floor or in a convenient mailbox at a nearby corner. No special arrangements are required to have a first-class letter picked up, nor will you have to make a trip to the post office to mail it.

Ask your local post office for a booklet entitled *Mailer's Guide* that describes the services USPS offers. If, for instance, your company is a nonprofit organization, special rates apply for sending bulk mail. Those lower rates come with conditions, which include packaging the mail in zip-code se-

*NOTE: Postal Service information is based on data provided by the United States Postal Service. If you work in another country, be sure to check with your post office to learn all the rules and services in your area.

quence. If your business sends out thousands of bills to customers, lower first-class rates can apply, provided the mail is packaged in a certain way. Your business can get a bulk-rate permit, which allows for the printing of bulk-rate indicia on an envelope or self-mailer (a folder, brochure, or catalog with an address label on the piece itself; self-mailers are not sent in envelopes). This saves having to affix a postage stamp to each piece.

If your company is large, the mailing department and others in the company are responsible for securing special permits, keeping up with changing postal regulations and rates, and preparing bulk mail according to USPS requirements. However, it is important for you to know about available USPS services. You can never predict when that knowledge will be useful.

USPS has several services you will probably use from time to time. To do so, you need to fill out USPS forms, available from a postal clerk at the post office. Get a sizable supply to fill them out at your desk rather than at the post office. You—or someone from the mail room—will have to take the letter or package with the completed forms to the post office when you want to mail it. You can type in the information asked for on the forms. If you make a mistake in the recipient's name and address on a multicopy form, such as Express Mail forms, retype a new form rather than erasing, since the third copy is the mailing label. To fill the form out by hand, use a ballpoint pen and press hard.

Express Mail

USPS Express Mail services were discussed in Chapter 6, but some explanation of the forms involved is needed. One form is a Post-Office-to-Post-Office Express Mail form, to be used if the addressee has a post office box. The box number should be included in the *"AT:"* section. The letter itself, or a notice indicating that the post office is holding the piece, will be placed in the recipient's box soon after the piece arrives in the post office. You may wish to call the addressee to alert him to watch for the piece since it will not be delivered to his office.

For an addressee without a post-office box, call to make sure he goes to the post office to pick up the piece. Usually, he can call ahead to the clerk at the Express Mail window to find out if the piece has arrived.

Another form arranges Post-Office-to-Addressee Express Mail. The USPS will deliver a piece sent with this form to the addressee.

Always keep your customer receipt copies of any Express Mail form. Put them in the file with the copy of the letter or forwarding memo you sent with the piece. If the piece does not arrive when scheduled, you will need to give the form number to the USPS in order to trace the whereabouts of the package. The USPS treats Express Mail in the same way it does certified mail, with some of the same paperwork, so the tracing procedures are well-defined: For a small extra charge, you can request a return receipt that shows you that the addressee has, in fact, received the piece.

The USPS has an Express Mail stamp, which carries the face value of the current basic rate for a Post-Office-to-Addressee delivery. If your piece is heavier than that allowed under the basic weight rate, you will have to have it weighed and rated individually at the post office or by your mail room.

Return Receipt

For registered, certified, insured, collect-on-delivery (COD), and Express Mail pieces, you can get a return receipt from USPS. This is a postcard form that is affixed to the envelope or package. The addressee must sign the card when it is delivered, and the USPS mails that card back to you as evidence that the package was delivered and actually received by the addressee or his agent.

You fill in the information on the front of the return-receipt form, typing or printing your own name and address and the additional items on the back. The postal clerk will fill in all costs for the service you choose: (a) show to whom and date delivered, (b) show address of delivery, or (c) restricted delivery to only the person who is named as the addressee. You fill in the type of service requested: (a) registered, (b) certified, (c) insured, (d) COD, or (e) Express Mail. You also fill in the form number from the registered, certified, insured, COD, or Express Mail form. This serves as a cross-check to insure that the proper piece was delivered and provides tracing information if needed.

The USPS has the person to whom the piece is delivered sign the form. The delivering post office writes in the date of delivery and places its stamp on the card, together with the initials of the postal employee who made the delivery. If the addressee refuses to accept delivery, that action is noted and both the card and the piece are returned to you.

When you use the return-receipt form, be sure to print or type "Return Receipt Requested" close to the "type of service" number on the front of the piece. (The type of service is either registered, certified, insured, COD, or Express Mail; the number identifies the form you use to designate that service.)

Registered Mail

Registered mail is the most secure method of sending letters through the USPS. It is carried in locked mail pouches and held in a post-office safe until delivery. The Post Office accepting a registered piece issues a registry number, which it enters on the form.

You fill in the bottom half of the registered mail form, giving the addressee's name and address and your own, plus the value of the article, if any, and whether you want postal insurance for it. The postal clerk fills in the top half of the form, indicating all charges for the services you request: registered fee, postage, special-delivery fee, return-receipt fee, restricted-delivery fee, special-handling fee, or airmail. Airmail is important if the piece is being sent overseas.

Since a registered piece is so important, you will usually request a return receipt along with registered service. Registered service is often used by companies that send jewelry or watches through the mail. Keep your copies of registered-mail forms and return receipts with the correspondence so you can prove shipment and delivery should any question arise in the future.

Certified Mail

Certified mail provides a receipt to the sender of a first-class letter and a record of delivery at the delivering post office. Unlike with registered mail, no insurance of the article is possible. The bottom block of the

Tip

Ask the post office for a booklet entitled *Mailer's Guide,* which describes the mail services the USPS offers.

receipt form with the form number and words "Certified Mail" is affixed to the article itself. If you are also requesting a return receipt, type or print the words "Return Receipt Requested" near this number.

You fill in the name and address of the addressee; the postal clerk fills in the charges for the services you request: postage, certified fee, special-delivery fee, and restricted-delivery fee. You keep the top portion of the form after the postal clerk has stamped it; it serves as your receipt. The number is to be used if tracing is required.

The USPS attaches a yellow form to the article. The addressee has to sign for the article, and the USPS keeps the yellow form as part of its record. If you have requested a return receipt, the addressee also has to sign the return receipt postcard form, which is mailed to you by the USPS.

Insured Mail

You can insure articles you send by USPS to either domestic or foreign destinations. Rates and limits can be obtained from a postal clerk. Articles of great value have a separate insured-mail form.

The postal clerk enters the charges on the top portion of the front of the form. The bottom portion—the form number and the words U.S. MAIL INSURED—is affixed to the article. If you are requesting a return receipt, print or type "Return Receipt Requested" on the piece near these numbers.

You fill in the name and address of the addressee on the back of the top portion of the form. After the postal clerk has stamped the form, keep it with any correspondence about the article. This part of the completed form is evidence of your being insured should you need to make a claim. Retain the form at least until you know the article has arrived safely.

On the insured-mail form for articles of limited value, fill in the back side of the form with the addressee's name and address. The postal clerk fills in the front of the form with charges for postage and fees, stamps the package or envelope INSURED and gives you the receipt. Retain the receipt until you are sure the package has arrived.

First-class, registered, COD, and Express Mail, as well as parcels, can all be insured. Certified mail cannot be insured.

Collect-on-Delivery (COD) Mail

If you mail an article being sold, and you want the addressee to pay the USPS for the purchase upon delivery, you can send the article COD. The USPS will, in turn, forward to you a money order in the amount collected from the addressee to pay for the article. You have set the price of the article. The addressee also has to pay COD handling charges and the fee for the money order. If the USPS has to return the article to you because the addressee has changed his mind about wanting the article and refuses to pay for it, you incur no extra charge since the possibility of such a refusal has been factored into the COD fee.

The COD form is a stiff tag with four perforated sections. The postal clerk puts the COD number on each of the four sections. The first or outermost section is your receipt. You fill in the name and address of the addressee and how much is due you for the article. The postal clerk fills in the charges: COD fee, postage, and any special-handling, special-delivery, restricted-delivery, or return-receipt fees. You usually do not need a return receipt with a COD article since payment in the form of USPS money order will be proof of receipt.

The second section is the Mailing Office Coupon. You fill in the name and address of the addressee and how much is due you for the article. The postal clerk fills in the rest. This coupon is retained by the sending post office for a year in case of any claim.

The third section, the Delivery Employee Coupon, is filled in by the delivering post office. It shows the date of delivery and whether the article was refused by the addressee. The coupon is retained by the delivering post office for two years in case of any claim.

The fourth or innermost section is the main mailing tag. You fill in the addressee's name and address as well as your own. The charges (funds to be sent to you) and the money-order fee are entered on the front of the section. You enter the charges and the post-office clerk enters the money-order fee. The back of the section is signed by the addressee when he receives the article and pays the charges. The money order covers only the charges. The money order and this section will be returned to you by the USPS as proof of delivery and as payment for the article.

Special Delivery

You can request special delivery or special handling of an article at the time you mail it. No special forms are required to secure either of these services. You can type SPECIAL DELIVERY on the envelope, or buy a rubber stamp bearing these words, or ask the postal clerk to stamp the words on the envelope when you mail it.

Special-delivery service is provided by the post office at the place of delivery. Service may include delivery at times beyond the normal delivery hours and Sunday and holiday delivery. The size of the local post office determines the extent of the special-delivery services.

Special Handling

Special-handling service is available for parcel-post packages only. It includes priority handling within the postal system so far as possible, but does not offer special delivery to the addressee from the delivering post office.

Customs Declarations

Many overseas countries require a customs declaration containing the contents and value of the package. The USPS uses two customs-declaration forms: a simple form for packages of modest value and a more complex form for parcel-post packages of greater value. The postal clerk will tell you which form to use, depending on the country to which you are mailing the article. The detailed rules governing customs declarations are continually shifting as individual countries change their laws and regulations. The USPS issues its postal clerks current guidelines, covering country-by-country requirements.

The International Postal Union has standardized postal customs-declaration forms, all of which now use French and English as the two world languages. You fill in the front with a brief description of the contents. Mark whether it is a gift or a sample, and indicate the value. Since you are sending the article from the United States, value is shown in U.S. dollars. Because many other countries also call their currency "dollars" and use the dollar sign ($), it is customary in international business to specify the kind of dollar (for example, US$ 15.90). Canada, (C$ 15.90), New Zealand (NZ$ 15.90), Australia (A$ 15.90), Hong Kong (HK$15.90), Singapore (S$ 15.90), and Malay (M$ 15.90) are among the many other places that use the dollar symbol.

It is especially important when sending an article to one of these "dollar" countries to specify US$ in your value declaration to avoid confusing the customs officer in the receiving country.

A more complex parcel-post customs-declaration form, produced by USPS for an article being posted from the United States, requests the value be shown in US$ amounts. The postal clerk fills in the information in the shaded boxes. When you have completed your sections of the form and the postal clerk has completed his and has stamped the form, tear off the first two copies and place them in the envelope (which is a part of the form kit). Peel off the cover of the back side of the form envelope, uncovering a sticky surface, and affix the envelope to the front of the package. The reason for the extra declaration forms is that different countries have different paperwork regulations for incoming parcels. This kit provides enough forms to meet the requirements of any country.

Zip-Code Directory

Every year, the USPS issues a zip-code directory, which contains all the zip codes in the country—in larger communities, by street and house or business number. You can purchase a copy of the USPS zip-code directory at any post office or from a Government Printing Office.

CHAPTER TWENTY-SEVEN

Secretarial Organizations and Associations

Secretaries have a number of professional organizations and associations. Many of these groups are national, with local chapters. Some are general in nature; others are related to specific specialties of secretarial work.

It's worthwhile to join one or more of these professional groups. Through membership you will meet secretaries from other firms, building your own "network" for future professional development. If you ever want to change jobs, someone you have met through a professional secretarial organization may be able to suggest a splendid, unadvertised opening at another company.

Membership will also provide opportunities to learn how to increase your professionalism. At meetings and seminars these groups sponsor, you will learn more about secretarial excellence. Professional organizations often publish newsletters, seminar reports, or books, and conduct courses that help enhance secretarial skills.

As we demand equal pay for equal work, secretarial salaries are under scrutiny. These organizations lobby at national, state, and industry levels for upgrading the pay and recognition due to secretaries. Whether you are female or male, you can only benefit as the job-enhancement efforts of these organizations succeed. The effectiveness of an organization's lobbying efforts depends partly on the size and scope of its membership. Your membership gives an organization a little more influence, which it will use to better the status of all secretaries.

Tip
   Through membership in a professional organization you will meet secretaries from other firms, building your own "network" for future professional development.

Congressional Staff Club
Box 2000, Longworth House Office Building, Washington, DC 20515
(202) 226-3250
   For secretarial and other employees of the U.S. Congress. Provides social and professional improvement programs. Weekly bulletin. Meeting: monthly.

The Creative Secretary
Executive Reports Corporation. 200 Old Tappan Road, Tappan, NJ 07632
(201) 767-5059
   A bimonthly newsletter for secretaries, filled with ideas, case studies, suggestions, and experiences of successful secretaries in many types and sizes of businesses.

Executive Women International
Spring Run Office Plaza, 965 E. 4800 Street, Suite 1, Salt Lake City, UT 84117
(801) 263-3296
   For women employed as executive secretaries or in administrative positions. Local chapters. Quarterly publication *(Times)*. Convention: annual.

National Association of Educational Office Personnel
7223 Lee Highway, Suite 301, Falls Church, VA 22046
(703) 533-0810
   For secretaries and others employed in offices of schools, colleges, universities, district and state departments of education. Local chapters. Provides professional training and summer institutes. Publications: quarterly journals and books. Convention: annual.

National Association of Executive Secretaries
900 S. Washington Street, #G 13, Falls Church, VA 22046
(703) 237-8616
   Dedicated to giving added stature and benefits to the executive secretary. Local chapters. Monthly magazine *(Exec—u-tary)*. Convention: annual.

National Association of Legal Secretaries (International)
2250 E. 73 Street, Suite 550, Tulsa, OK 74136
(918) 493-3540
   Sponsors legal secretarial training courses, leading to PLS (Professional Legal Secretary) certificate. Local chapters. Bimonthly publication *(The Docket)*. Convention: annual.

National Association of Rehabilitation Secretaries
633 S. Washington Street, Alexandria, VA 22314
(703) 836-0850
   Specializes in training and job potential for handicapped persons to serve as secretaries. Local chapters. Job service. Quarterly newsletter. Convention: annual.

Professional Secretaries International
301 E. Armour Boulevard, Kansas City, MO 64111
(816) 531-7010
   Professional organization of secretaries. Local chapters. Grants CPS certificate (Certified Professional Secretary) upon completion of professional examinations. Sponsors Secretaries Week. Provides education and professional development. Magazine 10/year *(The Secretary)*. Convention: annual.

Society of Architectural Administrators, c/o Deborah Worth. Henningson, Durham & Richardson, 11225 S.E. 6 Street, Building C, Suite 200, Bellevue, Washington 98004
(206) 453-1523

To advance the professionalism of secretaries employed by licensed architects. Local chapters. Quarterly journal *(Architectural Secretary)*. Convention: annual.

Visually Impaired Secretarial Transcribers Association (Blind)
600 N. Alabama Street, Tower 2, Apartment 2450, Indianapolis, IN 46204
(317) 635-4419

To protect and improve the training, employment, and related interests of visually impaired persons in secretarial work. Library and placement service. Newsletter. Convention: annual.

INDEX

A

Abbreviations, 155-59
   company names and organizations, 45, 156-57
   dates, 44
   English, 158
   geography and locations, 158
   Latin, 155-56, 158-59
   letter writing and, 44, 45
   metric, 158
   separating figures and, 147
   time, 158-59
   titles and forms of address, 157-58
Accuracy, business letters and, 51-52
   See also Editing documents; Proofreading
Agenda, meetings and, 117-18
Agreements, filing of, 123
Aide-mémoire, use of, 100
Air express service, 65, 66-67
   airlines and, 67-68
Air travel, 56-59
   agents and fares, 56-57
   boarding passes, 59
   clubs and bargains, 57-59
   frequent-flyer programs, 59
   meals, 59
   OAG and, 56
   reconfirmations and, 58
   VIP clubs, 58-59
   See also Reservations
Appearance and dress, secretary's, 22-23
   See also Clothes
Appearance of office (*See* Office appearance)
Appointments
   book and diary of, 95
   boss's calendar and, 36-37, 83-87. *See also* Calendar, boss's
   boss's juniors and, 86-87
   boss's peers and seniors and, 87
   confirming, 36
   courtesies and, 86, 95
   door guardianship and, 37-38, 94-95
   in-company visitors and, 37, 84, 86-87
   master calendar for, 36-37, 83-84, 96-97
   not previously made, 33-34
   open-door policy and, 94-95
   out-of-town visitors and, 38
   outside visitors, 84-85
   previously made, 33
   reception and, 33-37. *See also* Reception
   tentative, 85
   timing, 83, 84-85
   who makes, 36
   See also Visitors
Auto-dial phone system, 31-32
Automation (automated office), 126-33
   computer back-up procedures, 128
   computer consultants, 132
   disks, 128
   editing, software, 127
   LANS and, 128-29
   lighting and office furniture and, 130-34
   modems, 129-30
   new developments and publications, 133
   postage meters, 131
   records management and, 126-27
   service and assistance, 132
   shared equipment, 128-29
   time management and, 127
   training programs and courses, 132
   See also Computers; Word processors; specific kinds, problems, and uses

B

Banquet managers, reservations and, 60-62
Batteries, portable dictation and, 81
Boss's calendar. *See* Calendar, boss's
British English
   abbreviations in, 158
   overseas correspondence and, 51, 73-74
Business letters. *See* Letter writing
Business lunches, 62, 85
Business meetings. *See* Meetings

C

Calendar, boss's, 83-87
   appointments, 36-37, 83-87
   fifteen-minute segments, 84-85
   importance of time and, 83, 84, 85, 86

in-company visitors and, 84
master calendar, 36-37, 83-87, 96-97
outside visitors and, 84-85
tentative appointments and, 85
Call holding phone system, 31-32
Call waiting phone system, 31-32
Cars, rental of, 59-60
insurance and, 60
reservations, 60
Certified mail, 162-63
Clothes (dress), appearance and, 22-23, 91-93
choosing classics, 92-93
regional differences and standards, 91-93
success and, 91-93
Collect-on Delivery (COD) mail, 163-64
Commas, decreasing use of, 51-52, 80
Communications, internal electronic mail and, 68-69
Company names and organizations
abbreviations, 45, 156-57
location in correspondence, 44-45
"Company reputation," secretary's, 99
correspondence and, 41, 42
phone use and, 28
reception of visitors and, 22, 34
routine tasks and, 99
support of boss and, 34
Compound words, 148-54
words with prefixes, 153-54
Computers, 68-69, 126-33
back-up procedures, 128
consultants, 132
editing, software, 127
envelopes created on, 133
filters and, 130-31
information storage and retrieval and, 126-30
LANS and, 128-29
lighting and office furniture and, 130
memos and, 101
modems and, 129-30
naming documents and, 127
new developments, publications, 133
records management, 126-27
service and assistance, 132-33
training programs, 132, 133
See also Automation; Word processors
Concierges, hotel, 62-63
Conclusion, business letters and, 46
Conference calling phone system, 31

Confidential information, filing and disposing of, 123-24
Confidential (personal) mail, incoming, 39-40
Congressional Staff Club, address, 167
Contracts, filing of, 123
Copies and enclosures, correspondence and, 47, 80-81. *See also* Photocopiers
Correction (proofreader) marks, dictation and, 82
Correspondence, 39-52
categories, 40-41
dictation and. *See* Dictation
enclosures and copies, 47, 80-81
express services and, 64-69
faxing, 53-55
files (filing), 21, 41, 46, 47, 50, 121, 125
handwritten, 50
incoming, 39-42
international, 70-75. *See also* International correspondence
listing, 41
marking letters, use of colors, 41-42
memos, 100-5. *See also* Memos
outgoing, 42-52
personal (confidential), 39-40
printed material, 40
special reports and studies, 40-41
telegrams and electronic mail, 68-69
See also Letter writing
Couriers, use of, 165
Creative Secretary, The, 167
Cross-reference filing, 125
Customs declarations, postal forms for, 164-65

D

Dates (dating)
expressed in correspondence, 44, 51, 75
in memos, 102
Diaries, appointment, 95
Dictation, 78-82
batteries for portable units, 80
correction marks and, 82
distribution of copies, 81
electronic, 42-43, 78, 81
enclosures, 80-81
final form and, 80
letter writing and, 42-43. *See also* Letter writing

number of copies, 80
pool, 78
punctuation and, 80
reference needs and, 79
retention of original and, 80
soundalike words and, 81
word lists and, 78-79, 80, 81
   technical vocabulary and special word list
      and, 78-79
Dictionary, use of, 142, 144, 155
Disks, monitoring information on, 128
Dress and appearance, 22-23, 91-93. *See also*
   Clothes

E

Editing documents, 127. *See also* Accuracy;
   Proofreading
"Educated language," international correspondence and, 71
Electronic dictation, 42-43, 78, 81
Electronic mail, 68-69, 101
   internal, 68-69, 160
   memos and, 101
Emery & Purolater Courier, 66
Enclosures and copies, correspondence and, 47,
   80-81
English
   abbreviations, 158. *See also* Abbreviations
   as a second language, overseas correspondence
      and, 71-72
   spelling and, 140-44
   See also British English; Grammar and sen-
      tence structure
Entertainment
   hotel concierges and, 62-63
   reservations and, 62-63
   ticket agencies and, 62
Envelopes, computer-created, 133
Ergonomics, 130
Executive summaries, reports and, 107-9
Executive Women International, 167
Express Mail service, 64-65, 160, 161
Express services, 64-69
   airlines and, 67-68
   couriers and, 65
   Express Mail and, 64-65, 160, 161-62
   Federal Express, 66
   messengers and, 64-65

overnight air express, 66-67
telegrams and electronic mail, 68-69
UPS, 65-66
USPS forms, 161-62
Eyestrain, office lighting and, 130-31

F

Facsimile (fax) machines, 53-55
   directories, 54
   etiquette, 53-54
   "junk fax," 55
   logs of documents (paper trail), 54
   manual, 54
   on or off, 55
   paper supply monitoring, 54
   service and, 132
   specific company procedures and, 54
   timing and, 53
Federal Express, 66
File clerks, 124-25
Files (filing), 121-25
   appointments and, 36-37, 95
   automation and, 126-33
   changing, 122-23, 124
   confidential information, 123-24
   contracts and agreements, 123
   correspondence, 21, 41, 46, 47, 50, 121, 125
   cross-reference, 127
   fax numbers, 54
   file clerks and, 124-25
   financial statements, 123, 124
   "housekeeping," 123
   keeper of, 121
   learning, studying, 21, 122
   memos, 101, 121
   microfilming, 124
   as an ongoing record, 121-22
   phone numbers, 28
   respect for, 122
   space for, 124
   state abbreviations and, 45
   suggestions, 125
   systems, 121-22
   tickler, 97-98
   zip codes, 45
Filters, computer, 130-31
Financial statements, 113-16
   balance sheet, 113-16

filing, 123, 124
  meetings and, 118
  preparing, 113-16
  profit-and-loss (P/L) summary, 113, 116
  sections of, 113-16
  word processing and, 113-16
Foreign languages. *See* Language(s), international correspondence and
Formal language, international correspondence and levels of, 71, 72
Frequent-flyer programs, 59
Furniture, office, 130

G

Geography and locations, abbreviations for, 158
Gossip, 22
Grammar and sentence structure, 136-39
  active in place of passive voice, 136-37
  avoiding needless words, 137-38
  computer checkers and, 127
  language use and, 139
  misplaced antecedents and, 138-39
  paragraphs and main ideas and, 137
  positive statements and, 138
  users of English as a second language and, 71-73
  See also specific aspects, e.g., Compound words

H

Handwritten correspondence, 50
Headset, telephone, 32
Hold phone system, 31
Hotels, 60
  concierges, entertainment and, 62, 63
  frequent-traveler programs and, 60
  reservations, 60
Hyphenation. *See* Word division

I

Incoming mail, 39-41
  categories, 40-41
    highlighting subject matter or response requested, 41
  listing, 41
  marking, use of colors, 41-42
  personal (confidential), 39-40
  printed matter, 40
  routing, 39-40

  special reports and studies, 40-41
Information storage and retrieval
  back-up procedures, 128
  computers and, 126-30. *See also* Computers
  disks and, 128
  editing, software, 127
  LANS and, 128-29
  modems and, 129-30
  naming documents and, 127
Insured mail, 163
Intercoms, 31-32
International correspondence, 70-75
  British English and, 51, 73-74, 158
  characteristics of language use and, 70-71
  customs declarations postal forms, 164
  electronic mail and, 68
  Romance-language areas and, 72, 74-75
  sample letter, 74-75
  users of English as a second language and, 71-73. *See also* Language(s), international correspondence and
  USPS forms, 160-65. *See also* Mail(ing)
  See also Letter writing
Interviews. *See* Job interview

J

Job description, secretarial, 17
Job interview, secretarial, 17

L

Language(s), international correspondence and, 70-75
  English as a second language and, 71-73
  level for business correspondence, 71
  levels of education and, 71
  levels of formality and, 71, 72
  Romance languages and, 72, 74-75
  sending and receiving and, 71-72
  technical words and, 73
  See also Letter writing; specific aspects, kinds, problems
Latin abbreviations, 155-56, 158-59
Legal documents, filing of, 123
Legal terms spellers, 142
Letter writing, 39-52, 135, 136-39, 140-44, 145-47, 148-51, 155-59
  abbreviations and, 45, 155-59. *See also* Abbreviations

accuracy, checking, and style, 50, 51-52
body of the letter, 46, 75
compound words and, 148-54
conclusion, complimentary closings, 46, 75
copies and enclosures, 47, 86-87
"correct" style and, 51
dates, expressing, 44, 51, 75
dictation and, 78-82. *See also* Dictation
dictator/secretary initials, 47
express services and, 64-69, 161-62
filing copies, 21, 41, 46, 47, 50, 121, 125
first copy as draft copy, 79
first copy as final copy, 79
grammar and sentence structure and, 136-39.
   See also Grammar and sentence structure
handwritten, 50
international correspondence, 70-75
   See also International correspondence
language(s) and. *See* Language(s)
mailing. *See* Mail(ing)
name, title, company address, and city, 44-45
personal notes added, 49
proofreading, 50, 51-52
punctuation and, 50-51, 82
salutation, 45-46
samples, 48, 49, 74
signature and, 46-47, 50-51
spelling and, 140-44
titles of address, 44, 45-46, 75, 157-58
typing and, 43-44. *See also* Typing
word division and, 145-47
word processors and, 43-44, 78, 79, 80
zip codes, 45, 66, 67, 165
See also Correspondence
Lighting, office, 130-31
Local-area networks (LANS), 128-29
Locations, abbreviations for, 158
Loyalty, 21-22
   office politics and, 21-22
Lunches, business. *See* Business lunches

M

Mail(ing)
   electronic, 68-69, 101, 160
   express services and, 64-69
   postage meters, charts, and scales, 131
   Postal Service forms, 160-65
   U.S. Postal Service, 160-65
   See also Correspondence; Letter writing; specific kinds, e.g., Insured mail
Mailer's Guide, 160
Manual of Style, A, 148
Master calendar, 83-84, 96-97
   appointments and, 36-37, 83-84
   routines and, 96-97
   See also Calendar, boss's
Meals (diet, food), 59, 60-62
   air travel reservations and, 59
   restaurant reservations and, 60-62
   See also Business lunches
Medical terms spellers, 142
Meetings (business meetings), 117-20
   agenda for, 117-18, 119
   announcements of, 117-18
   attendees, 117, 120
   copies of proceedings, 120
   follow-up, 120
   minutes of, 119-20
   note-taking at 119-20
   physical arrangements, 118-19, 120
   reports and financial statements, 118
   secretary's presence at, 119-20
   thank-you notes following, 120
Memos, 100-5, 135
   body of, 102
   copies, 101, 102
   dating, 102
   direct style for, 100
   elements in, 102
   file copies, 101
   forms for, 101
   from/to, 102
   samples, 103-5
   secretary's, 101, 102-3
   subject of, 102
   types, 100-1
   See also Correspondence; Letter writing
Messages, telephone, 27-28
Messenger service, 64-65
Metric abbreviations, 158
Microfilming of files, 124
Modems, 129-30
   receiving information, 129-30
   sending information, 129
Mute phone system, 31

N

Names, personal, overseas correspondence and, 75
  See also Titles and forms of address
Names of companies and organizations
  abbreviations for, 156-57
  location in correspondence of, 44-45
  See also Titles and forms of address
National Association of Educational Office Personnel, address, 167
National Association of Legal Secretaries (International), address, 167
National Association of Rehabilitation Secretaries, address, 167
Note pads, 101
Notes (notepaper), daily reminders and use of, 98-99

O

Office appearance (environment, workplace), 88-90
  desktop (paperwork management), 89
  lighting and furniture, 130-31
  office cleaners and maintenance department, 90
Office politics, loyalty and, 21-22
Official Airlines Guide (OAG), 56
Overseas correspondence. *See* International correspondence

P

Parcels (packages)
  air-express service and, 64, 66-67
  airlines and, 67-68
  couriers and, 65
  express services and, 64-69
  messengers and, 64-65
  UPS and, 65-66
  USPS forms for, 160-65
Personal (confidential) mail, incoming, 39, 40
Personal names, overseas correspondence and, 75.
  See also Titles and forms of address
Photocopiers (photocopies), 80, 131-32
  copier logs and, 131-32
  file copies and, 124
  letter writing and, 43
Pool dictation, 78

Postage charts, 131
Postage meters, automated, 131
Postage scales, 131
Postal Service, U.S. *See* U.S. Postal Service
Post office box numbers, overseas correspondence and, 75
Posture and back pain, office furniture and lighting and, 130
Presentation folders, reports and, 111-12
Professional Secretaries International, address, 167
Proofreading
  accuracy in correspondence and, 50, 51-52
  computers and word processors and, 127
  correction marks and dictation and, 82
  electronic checks for spelling errors, 43-44, 127, 144
Punctuation
  correspondence and, 44, 51-52, 80
  decreasing use of commas, 51-52, 80
  dictation and, 80
  usage manuals, 80

R

Radio Corporation of America (RCA), overseas message traffic and, 68
Reception, 33-38
  company visitors and, 37
  confirming appointments, 36
  door guardianship and, 37-38, 94-95
  kinds of visits, appointments and, 33-36
  making appointments and, 36
  master appointment calendar and, 36-37, 83-84
  out-of-town visitors and, 38
Records management, automation and, 126-27, 132
  See also Automation; Computers; Word processors
Redial phone system, 31-32
Registered mail, 162
Reminder systems, routines and, 97-99
  daily notes and, 98-99
  memos and, 100-5
  tickler file and, 97-99
  use of color and, 97
Rental cars, 59-60
  insurance and, 60
  reservations and, 60
Reports (report writing), 101, 106-12, 135

executive summaries, 107-9
filing, 123
main body of, 109-10
meetings and, 118
presentation folders for, 111-12
spacing, 110
table of contents, 110-11
title page, 106-7
See also Letter writing
Research reports. *See* Reports
Reservations, 56-63
  agents and fares, 56-58
  air travel and, 56-59. *See also* Air travel
  business lunches and, 62
  car-rental, 60
  entertainment, 62-63
  hotels, 60
  reconfirmations, 58
  restaurants, 60-62
  theater, 62-63
  travel, 56-57
Restaurants, 60-62
  reservations, 60-62
Return receipt mail, 162, 163
Romance-language areas, overseas correspondence and, 72, 74-75
Routines (routine tasks), 96-97
  daily notes and, 98-99
  master calendar and, 96-97. *See also* Master calendar
  memos and, 100-5
  planning, scheduling, and schedule monitoring and, 96-97
  reminder suggestions, 97-99. *See also* Reminder systems
  tickler file and, 97-98

S

Salutations, letter writing and, 45-46
Secretarial organizations and associations, listed, 166-68
Secretary (secretarial role), 15, 16-23
  basic guidelines, 15, 16-23
  boss's concept of relationship with, 17, 18
  company policies and procedures and, 19-20
  "company reputation" and. *See* "Company reputation"
  dictation and. *See* Dictation
  interviewing for, 17

job description and, 17
  learning the boss's job and, 20-21
  learning the company's mission and, 18-19
  loyalty, gossip, appearance and dress and, 21-23, 92-93
  organizations and associations, listed, 166-68
  role definitions, 16-17
  studying the files and, 21
  training courses and programs, 132
Shredding files, 123-24
Society of Architectural Administrators, address, 168
Soundalike words, dictation and, 81
Speakerphone, 31-32
Special delivery mail, 164
Special handling mail, 164
Speed-dial phone system, 31-32
Speller-divider books, 142, 144, 145-46, 147
Spelling, 140-44
  compound words, 148-54
  dictation and, 79
  electronic checks for errors, 43-44, 127, 147
  letter writing (correspondence) and, 43-44, 51, 140-44
  plurals and, 141, 142-43
  problem areas, 142-44
  wordbooks (spellers) for, 142, 144, 145-46, 147
State abbreviations, 45, 158

T

Task lighting, 131
Technical words
  abbreviations and, 155
  dictation and, 78, 79
  international correspondence and, 73
  legal and medical, 142
Telegrams, 68
Telephone use, 26-32
  answering, 27
  complex phone systems, 31-32
  ending calls, 30-31
  fax numbers and, 54
  getting the number right, 30
  headset, 32
  interrupting the boss for a call, 28-29
  listing regularly called numbers, 28
  list of calls, 28
  making outgoing calls, 29

managing voice mail (computerized answering machine), 31, 126
manner and technique, 26-27
messages, forms, pads, 27-28
"on hold," 31
power game and, 29-30
service and assistance, 132
telegrams and electronic mail and, 68
transferring calls, 30, 31-32
Theater reservations, 62-63
Ticket agencies, entertainment and, 62
Tickler file, 97-98
Time, abbreviations for, 158-59
Time management, 130, 132
Titles and forms of address, letter writing and, 44, 75, 157-58
abbreviations, 157-58
in overseas correspondence, 75
in salutations, 45-46
Titles of reports, 106-7
Training courses and programs, 132, 133
Travel reservations, 56-63
agents and fares, 56-58
rental cars and, 59-60
See also Air travel
Typing (typewriters), 126
financial statements and, 113-16
letter writing and, 43-44. *See also* Letter writing
memos and, 100-5
reports and, 106-12

U

United Parcel Service (UPS), 65-66
U.S. Postal Service (USPS), 160-65
bulk-rate mail, 160-61
certified mail, 162
COD mail, 163-64
customs declarations, 164-65
Express Mail, 64-65, 161-62
forms, 160-65
insured mail, 163
registered mail, 162-63
return receipt mail, 162, 163
special delivery mail, 164
special handling mail, 164
zip-code directory, 165

V

VIP airline clubs, 58-59
Visitors, 33-38, 94-95
courtesies and, 86, 95
diary of, 95
door guardianship and, 37-38, 94-95
entertainment and, 62-63
in-company, 37, 84, 86-87
kinds, appointments and, 33-36. *See also* Appointments
open-door policy and, 94-95
out-of-town, 38, 86
outside, 84-85
receptionist and, 33
reception of, 33-38, 94-95. *See also* Reception
reservations and, 56-63. *See also* Reservations
timing and, 83, 84-86, 94
Visually Impaired Secretarial Transcribers Association (Blind), address, 168
Voice mail (computerized answering machine), 31, 126

W

Western Union (WU), 68
Word division (hyphenation), 51, 145-47
basic rules, pronunciation and, 145, 146-47
compound words, 148-54
personal names and, 147
Word lists (vocabulary)
abbreviations, 155-59
compound words, 148-54
dictation and letter writing and, 79, 80, 81
soundalike words, 81
See also spelling; Word division
Word processors, 126-27
editing, software, 127
financial statements and, 113-16
letter writing and, 43-44, 78, 79, 80
numerical logs and, 127
records management and, 126-27
service and assistance, 132-33
spelling checkers and, 43-44, 127, 147
word division and, 145-47

Z

Zip codes, 45
express service and, 66, 67
letter writing and, 45, 165
USPS directory, 165